Pietro Bembo
A Life in Laurels and Scarlet

LEGENDA

LEGENDA is the Modern Humanities Research Association's book imprint for new research in the Humanities. Founded in 1995 by Malcolm Bowie and others within the University of Oxford, Legenda has always been a collaborative publishing enterprise, directly governed by scholars. The Modern Humanities Research Association (MHRA) joined this collaboration in 1998, became half-owner in 2004, in partnership with Maney Publishing and then Routledge, and has since 2016 been sole owner. Titles range from medieval texts to contemporary cinema and form a widely comparative view of the modern humanities, including works on Arabic, Catalan, English, French, German, Greek, Italian, Portuguese, Russian, Spanish, and Yiddish literature. Editorial boards and committees of more than 60 leading academic specialists work in collaboration with bodies such as the Society for French Studies, the British Comparative Literature Association and the Association of Hispanists of Great Britain & Ireland.

The MHRA encourages and promotes advanced study and research in the field of the modern humanities, especially modern European languages and literature, including English, and also cinema. It aims to break down the barriers between scholars working in different disciplines and to maintain the unity of humanistic scholarship. The Association fulfils this purpose through the publication of journals, bibliographies, monographs, critical editions, and the MHRA Style Guide, and by making grants in support of research. Membership is open to all who work in the Humanities, whether independent or in a University post, and the participation of younger colleagues entering the field is especially welcomed.

ALSO PUBLISHED BY THE ASSOCIATION

Critical Texts
Tudor and Stuart Translations • *New Translations* • *European Translations*
MHRA Library of Medieval Welsh Literature

MHRA Bibliographies
Publications of the Modern Humanities Research Association

The Annual Bibliography of English Language & Literature
Austrian Studies
Modern Language Review
Portuguese Studies
The Slavonic and East European Review
Working Papers in the Humanities
The Yearbook of English Studies

www.mhra.org.uk
www.legendabooks.com

THE FONDATION BARBIER-MUELLER

The Fondation Barbier-Mueller pour l'étude de la poésie italienne de la Renaissance was created in 1997 through the initiative and generosity of Jean Paul Barbier-Mueller, whose collections of primitive art are known worldwide. Housed in the University of Geneva, it offers scholars free and easy access to an exceptionnal collection of more than six hundred books of Italian poetry printed between 1480 and 1620, most of them very rare. The Foundation's aim is to promote and stimulate research on dozens of poets, often little known, who, in the wake of Petrarch, explored new paths in creative writing and had a wide influence on European sensibility and literature in the Early modern era.

The Foundation edits a journal, *Italique*, and a series of scholarly editions and essays, *Textes et Travaux de la Fondation Barbier-Mueller*, both with Editions Droz in Geneva. There is a scientific catalogue of the collection compiled by Jean Balsamo, *De Dante à Chiabrera. Poètes italiens dans la bibliothèque de la Fondation Barbier-Mueller*, Genève, Droz, 2007, 2 vols. The website www.fondation-italienne-barbier-mueller.org provides an inventory of the books as well as digitised documents.

Pietro Bembo

A Life in Laurels and Scarlet

Marco Faini

Translated by Viviane Lowe

Modern Humanities Research Association
in association with the
Fondation Barbier-Mueller pour l'étude de la poésie italienne de la Renaissance
2016

Published by Legenda
an imprint of the Modern Humanities Research Association
Salisbury House, Station Road, Cambridge CB1 2LA

ISBN 978-1-78188-441-6

First published 2017

All rights reserved. No part of this publication may be be reproduced or disseminated or transmitted in any form or by any means, electronic, mechanical, photocopying, recording or otherwise, or stored in any retrieval system, or otherwise used in any manner whatsoever without written permission of the copyright owner, except in accordance with the provisions of the Copyright, Designs and Patents Act 1988, or under the terms of a licence permitting restricted copying issued in the UK by the Copyright Licensing Agency Ltd, Saffron House, 6–10 Kirby Street, London EC1N 8TS, England, or in the USA by the Copyright Clearance Center, 222 Rosewood Drive, Danvers MA 01923. Application for the written permission of the copyright owner to reproduce any part of this publication must be made by email to legenda@mhra.org.uk.

Disclaimer: Statements of fact and opinion contained in this book are those of the author and not of the editors or the Modern Humanities Research Association. The publisher makes no representation, express or implied, in respect of the accuracy of the material in this book and cannot accept any legal responsibility or liability for any errors or omissions that may be made.

Trademark notice: Product or corporate names may be trademarks or registered trademarks, and are used only for identification and explanation without intent to infringe.

© Fondation Barbier-Mueller pour l'étude de la poésie italienne de la Renaissance 2017

Copy-Editor: Richard Correll

Iconography: Caroline Gibert

CONTENTS

	Acknowledgements	ix
	Prologue: An Altercation on the Rialto	1
1	By the Hand of a Great Master	6
2	'To rise above the common mud': The Dream of Literature	16
3	This Sacred Lead	29
4	Three Women Seated around the Heart	43
5	At the Court of the Queen of Cyprus	59
6	The Carnival of Venus	71
7	Roman Sensualities	85
8	The Common Father of Letters	97
9	Writing Sonnets in the College: The Amorous Cardinal Bembo	105
	Bibliographical Note	117
	Index	123

ACKNOWLEDGEMENTS

The author wishes to thank Moreno Berva, Massimo Danzi, Nicolas Ducimetière, Caroline Gibert, Chiara Lastraioli, Viviane Lowe, Graham Nelson. A special and heartfelt thank goes to Michel Jeanneret for his enthusiasm, support and advice.

M.F., Cambridge, 2016

LIST OF ILLUSTRATIONS

Fig. 1. Francesco Guardi, *The Grand Canal, Venice, with the Palazzo Bembo*, c. 1768, oil on canvas, 47 × 76.5 cm, J. Paul Getty Museum, Los Angeles. Digital image courtesy of the Getty's Open Content Program

Fig. 2. Copy after Raphael, *Portrait of Giuliano de' Medici*, sixteenth century, tempera and oil on canvas, 83.2 × 66 cm, The Metropolitan Museum of Art, New York. The Jules Bache Collection, 1949/www.metmuseum.org

Fig. 3. *Mensa Isiaca* or *Tabula bembina*, first century CE, bronze tablet, 142.24 × 91.44 cm, Museo Egizio, Turin. Photo Scala, Florence/FMAE, Torino

Fig. 4. Valerio Belli, *Medal of Pietro Bembo*, c. 1532, bronze, diameter 4 cm, Victoria and Albert Museum, London. © Victoria and Albert Museum, London

Fig. 5. Giulio Bonasone, *Portrait of Pietro Bembo*, 1572, engraving, 23.3 × 17 cm, Metropolitan Museum of Art, New York. Rogers Fund, 1922/www.metmuseum.org

Fig. 6. Titian, *Portrait of Pietro Bembo*, c. 1540, oil on canvas, 94.5 × 76.5 cm, National Gallery of Art, Washington. Samuel H. Kress Collection/Courtesy National Gallery of Art, Washington

Fig. 7. Domenico Ghirlandaio, *Scenes from the Life of St Francis: Confirmation of the Franciscan Rule by Pope Honorius III*, c. 1482–85, fresco, Sassetti Chapel, basilica of Santa Trinita, Florence (detail: Angelo Poliziano). © 2015. Photo Scala, Florence

Fig. 8. Pietro Bembo, *Petri Bembi De Ætna ad Angelum Chabrielem liber,* Impressus Venetiis, in ædibus Aldi Romani mense februario MVD, c. Air, Cambridge University Library. Reproduced by the kind permission of the Syndics of Cambridge University Library (4.B.3.134 [4580])

Fig. 9. Pietro Bembo, *Le cose volgari di messer Francesco Petrarcha*, Impresso in Vinegia nelle case d'Aldo Romano, nel anno M D I del mese di Luglio, c. Ai r, Bibliothèque nationale de France, Paris. Bibliothèque nationale de France

Fig. 10. Pietro Bembo, *Le cose volgari di messer Francesco Petrarcha*, Impresso in Vinegia nelle case d'Aldo Romano, nel anno M D I del mese di Luglio, c. Ziii r, Bibliothèque nationale de France, Paris. Bibliothèque nationale de France

Fig. 11. Raphael, *Portrait of Fedra Inghirami*, 1514–16, oil on wood, 89.5 × 62.8 cm, Galleria Palatina, Florence. Photo Scala, Florence — courtesy of the Ministero the Ministero Beni e Att. Culturali

Fig. 12. Bartolomeo Veneto, *Portrait of a Gentleman*, c. 1512, oil on wood, 73.5 × 53 cm, Galleria Nazionale d'Arte antica, Rome. Photo Scala, Florence — courtesy of the Ministero Beni e Att. Culturali

Fig. 13. Lucrezia Borgia's hair (1480–1519), 1928. Veneranda Pinacoteca Ambrosiana, Milan. © Veneranda Biblioteca Ambrosiana/DeAgostini Picture Library/Scala, Florence

Fig. 14. Pinturicchio, *St Catherine's Disputation*, 1492–94, Apostolic Palace, Borgia Apartments, Vatican (detail: presumed portrait of Lucrezia Borgia). © 2015 Photo Scala, Florence

Fig. 15. Lorenzo Costa, *Allegory of the Court of Isabella d'Este*, sixteenth century, oil on canvas, 164.5 × 197.5 cm, Musée du Louvre, Paris. Photo © RMN-Grand Palais (Musée du Louvre) / Thierry Le Mage

Fig. 16. Pietro Bembo, *Gli Asolani di Messer Pietro Bembo*, Venice, Aldus, 1505, f. 1 r°. First edition. Fondation Barbier-Mueller pour l'étude de la poésie italienne de la Renaissance, University of Geneva. Photo: Fondation Barbier-Mueller pour l'étude de la poésie italienne de la Renaissance, University of Geneva

Fig. 17. Lorenzo Lotto, *Assumption of the Virgin*, 1506, oil on wood, 175 × 162 cm, Duomo, Asolo. © Electa/Leemage

Fig. 18. Gentile Bellini, *Caterina Cornaro, Queen of Cyprus*, c. 1500, tempera on canvas, 63 × 49 cm, Szepmueveszeti Muzeum, Budapest. Foto: Razso Andras © 2015. The Museum of Fine Arts Budapest/Scala, Florence

Fig. 19. Giorgione, *Ritratto Ludovisi*, early sixteenth century, oil on canvas, 76.3 × 63.4 cm, Museo di Palazzo Venezia, Rome. © 2015. Photo Scala, Florence — courtesy of the Ministero Beni e Att. Culturali

Fig. 20. Titian, *Portrait of Eleonora Gonzaga Della Rovere*, 1536–38, oil on canvas, 114 × 103 cm, Uffizi Gallery, Florence. Photo Scala, Florence — courtesy of the Ministero Beni e Att. Culturali

Fig. 21. Titian, *Portrait of Francesco Maria Della Rovere, Duke of Urbino*, 1536, oil on canvas, 114 × 103 cm, Uffizi Gallery, Florence. © 2015 Photo Scala, Florence — courtesy of the Ministero Beni e Att. Culturali

Fig. 22. [*Triumph of Priapus*], in Francesco Colonna, *Hypnerotomachia Poliphili*, Venice, Aldus, 1499, f. 98 r°. First edition. Fondation Martin Bodmer, Cologny, Geneva (Inc. B. 77). Fondation Martin Bodmer, Cologny, Geneva

Fig. 23. Raphael, *Triumph of Galatea*, 1511–12, fresco, Villa Farnesina, Rome. © 2015. Photo Scala, Florence

Fig. 24. Raphael, *St Catherine of Alexandria*, c. 1507, oil on wood, 71 × 55 cm, National Gallery, London. © 2015. Copyright The National Gallery, London/Scala, Florence

Fig. 25. Michelangelo, *Bacchus*, 1497, marble, height 203 cm, Museo Nazionale del Bargello, Florence. © 2015. Photo Scala, Florence — courtesy of the Ministero Beni e Att. Culturali

Fig. 26. Raphael, *Double portrait (Andrea Navagero and Agostino Bevazzano)*, c. 1516, oil on canvas, 76 × 107 cm, Doria Pamphilj Gallery, Rome. Amministrazione Doria Pamphilj srl con socio unico

Fig. 27. *Le Prose del Bembo,* Florence, Lorenzo Torrentino, Stampatore ducale, 1548, title page. Fondation Barbier-Mueller pour l'étude de la poésie italienne de la Renaissance, University of Geneva. Fondation Barbier-Mueller pour l'étude de la poésie italienne de la Renaissance, University of Geneva

Fig. 28. Sebastiano del Piombo, *Portrait of Cardinal Reginald Pole*, c. 1540, oil on canvas, 112 × 95 cm, Hermitage Museum, Saint Petersburg. © 2015. Photo Fine Art Images/Heritage Images/Scala, Florence

Fig. 29. Michelangelo, *Conversion of Saul*, 1542–45, fresco, Pauline Chapel, Vatican. © 2015 Photo Scala, Florence

Fig. 30. Michelangelo, *Crucifixion of St Peter*, 1545–50, fresco, Pauline Chapel, Vatican. © 2015 Photo Scala, Florence

Fig. 31. Titian, *Martyrdom of St Lawrence*, c. 1548–57, oil on canvas, 493 × 277 cm, church of Santa Maria Assunta dei Gesuiti, Venice. © 2015 Cameraphoto/Scala, Florence

PROLOGUE

An Altercation on the Rialto

Venice, some time in the year 1487. Clutching a sheaf of documents, a young man strides hurriedly toward the law courts. His father Bernardo is on business in Rome and has asked him to represent him in a lawsuit against a certain Simon Goro. It so happens that today Simon, too, is otherwise engaged and has sent his nephew Giusto in his place. The choice is ill-advised: the nephew is a worthless *pazzerone*, an idle good-for-nothing. This morning, his evil genius inspires him to play a prank on the young man who is hurrying toward him. Taking the latter by surprise, Giusto snatches the documents and runs away. Dismayed, the young man stops in his tracks, but, realising there is nothing he can do, he turns toward home. Upon reaching the Rialto, however, he runs into Giusto again. Venice is a small city, as everyone knows — even today one is forever running into the same people. All around them, people crowd the stalls of the apothecaries and spice merchants, buying and selling, or sit on benches in front of printers' workshops, browsing recent publications or perusing new folios straight from the press. The curious and enterprising Venetians are intrigued by this art, brought to the city by a German, Giovanni da Spira, in 1469, almost twenty years ago. By a strange and wonderful coincidence, Bernardo's son, Pietro, was born the following year. Decades later, grown famous thanks to this invention, Pietro, who firmly believed in premonitions, fate and omens, may have reflected on this conjunction, which looked very much like predestination. At the time of the episode recounted here, however, all that is far in the future. For now, there is only the sneering ne'er-do-well Giusto — the name is such a poor fit that it seems almost sarcastic — who continues to taunt his young rival. Pietro Bembo, by contrast, is the son of an ambassador of the Republic. Giusto cannot be allowed to get away with such behaviour, and Pietro has no intention of tolerating it. The crowd, sensing what is about to happen, quickly steps back to form a circle around the antagonists.

Meanwhile, leaning out of the triple-arched window of her Gothic-Byzantine palace on the Grand Canal, the offended party's mother, the noble Venetian lady Elena Marcello, impatiently awaits her son's return. The night before, she dreamed that he was wounded on the Rialto, and now she does not see him anywhere. From the balcony of the main floor she can see the bridge — it is almost close enough to touch — but the piazza opposite is hidden from view [Figure 1].

The gondolas glide silkily under the bridge, covered with their distinctive *felze*, a sort of awning that shields the Venetians' thousand mysteries from prying eyes.

Fig. 1. Francesco Guardi, *The Grand Canal, Venice, with the Palazzo Bembo, c.* 1768, oil on canvas, 47 × 76.5 cm, J. Paul Getty Museum, Los Angeles. Digital image courtesy of the Getty's Open Content Program

Moored to the dolphins, boats of all kinds — *bragozzi, burchi, rasconi* — rock placidly, sails furled, pennants emblazoned with the lion of Saint Mark lazily fluttering in the breeze. A swarm of rowers, sailors and porters busy themselves with oars, rigging and cables, and load or offload every variety of merchandise.

The Grand Canal responds to Elena's apprehension with bustling and indifferent tranquillity. Elena also dreamed of the name of her son's aggressor; without a doubt, it was a prophetic dream. Did she not warn Pietro several times this morning to be on his guard? But Pietro Bembo, though not yet twenty, is tall and well built, strong and agile. And he is not without courage. Moving away from the Rialto crowd, the two young men draw their weapons. Giusto, wielding a short, curved sword called a *storta*, takes advantage of his left-handedness to wound his adversary in the hand, almost severing his forefinger; in later years, it never fully recovers its dexterity.

Many years later, in a letter of 26 February 1502 to Giuliano de' Medici — known as 'il Magnifico Giuliano' — Pietro would recall this incident with amusement, as if boasting of a youthful adventure. A famous womaniser and gifted poet, Lorenzo's youngest son first met Pietro Bembo in 1499 and became his close friend during the unforgettable years they spent together at the court of Urbino. Nine years younger than Pietro (Giuliano was born on 12 March 1479, Pietro on 20 May 1470), he knew exactly what his friend was referring to. He too had been an impudent child and as a boy had taken to roaming the streets of his native city late at night, imagining himself as the keeper of its peace. If anyone aroused his suspicion, he did not hesitate to call on the man to state his name. By a strange coincidence, one night, when he was barely fourteen, Giuliano had the misfortune of challenging the wrong man,

Fig. 2. Copy after Raphael, *Portrait of Giuliano de' Medici*, sixteenth century, tempera and oil on canvas, 83.2 × 66 cm, The Metropolitan Museum of Art, New York. The Jules Bache Collection, 1949/www.metmuseum.org

who attacked and wounded him, slicing off the last phalange of his left forefinger. The mutilated finger is clearly visible in a very beautiful portrait of Giuliano after a lost original by Raphael, which now hangs in the Metropolitan Museum of Art in New York [Figure 2].

Another famous figure whose story would later intersect with Pietro's, the writer Pietro Aretino — less a friend than a respected, perhaps even feared, rival — was also wounded in the hand. In his case, however, this was not the consequence of an unexpected altercation or unfortunate encounter but a premeditated ambush. His aggressor, Achille Della Volta, was an emissary of the powerful *datario*, Cardinal Giovan Matteo Giberti, who was attempting in this way to settle a number of accounts at the court of Pope Clement VII. The attack was perpetrated in 1525. The sack of Rome in 1527, and the widespread destruction wreaked by the imperial troops, put an end to Giberti's intrigues. Aretino, meanwhile, had fled to Venice.

Though unrelated, these three incidents involved three equally headstrong men, three passionate, irrepressible writers who were particularly liable to the sting and bite of Eros. All three were central figures of the late Renaissance and familiar with the Italian courts before their collapse.

As a youth, Pietro was already in many ways the man he would become later in life: keenly aware of his rank and value, proud and quick to take offence. Quick, also, to feel slighted. Age and experience at court — especially the court of Rome, which caused his friend and contemporary Ludovico Ariosto great unease — taught him prudence, but his dislike of injustice remained just as intense. According to his biographer, the prelate and poet Ludovico Beccadelli, 'Messer Pietro had a sweet, guileless nature, but it is true that he could be spiteful, especially when he felt he had suffered injury without good cause, and for that reason he renounced the friendship of many great lords at the court of Rome.'

The nobility of his character also transpired in many aspects of his behaviour. According to the biographers who knew him personally, he loved to spend liberally and surrounded himself with friends and trusted servants. Yet Pietro's generosity is somewhat debatable: though capable of great liberality, he was also very close with his money. Despite those ambiguities, he clearly possessed admirable qualities of generosity and congeniality. That penchant incited him to recognise and reward, sometimes far beyond their real merit, the qualities of those who approached him. He distinguished himself by his natural inclination to friendship and his gift for nurturing relationships. These qualities were complemented by a remarkable intelligence and grace in conversation: 'He was admirable, too, in his way of living, which was characterised by a true geniality and beautiful delicacy; his speech was gentle, and his habits amiable and peaceful, like his entire way of life. If one adds to this an intelligence of extraordinary nature and power, one may easily understand why he was so well loved, and by so many.' That was how the author of *Galateo*, Monsignor Giovanni Della Casa, remembered Pietro: a charming man, born to win the hearts of all who met him. Indeed, he succeeded not only in earning the admiration of most scholars, but also charmed courtiers of both sexes with his highly sophisticated writing. After the publication of his dialogues, 'all of Italy started to read and study *Gli Asolani* so avidly that anyone who did not know its argument was considered utterly lacking in urbanity and elegance'. However, we know that this engaging and affable conversationalist, talented writer and consummate courtier was also a deeply solitary man, who sought, whenever possible, to 'bury himself in books'. Moreover, before achieving literary and worldly fame, Pietro suffered his share of bitter disappointment, misfortune and pain, including an assassination attempt at the hand of his nephew. Devotee of the Muses and hunter of generous commissions, solitary ascetic and wily court operator — including at the court of Rome, the most treacherous of all — cardinal of the Church and lover of Lucrezia Borgia and Morosina, whose name the prudish Giovanni Della Casa blushed to write, true believer in the sanctity of friendship and vindictive polemicist: Pietro was all these men at once. The contradictions were no doubt intrinsic to the man, but they also reflected a culture in rapid flux at a time of intense social, political and religious upheaval.

Fig. 3. *Mensa Isiaca* or *Tabula bembina*, first century CE, bronze tablet, 142.24 × 91.44 cm, Museo Egizio, Turin. Photo Scala, Florence/FMAE, Torino

CHAPTER 1

By the Hand of a Great Master

Padua, 1537. The youth is now an old man. Soon he will be seventy. His hair is thinner. But his mind, tempered by the fire of brilliant successes and harrowing losses, is as sharp as ever, his desires as intense. Pietro Bembo is restless. Finally, the most famous goldsmith alive is to pay him a visit. Finally, he will receive the medal engraved with his portrait that he so ardently desires. His friend Valerio Belli designed a first medal for him five years ago. Now, gazing at it, weighing it in his hand, turning it between his fingers, he finds it lacking, and recalls that he was never truly satisfied with it. Trembling with barely contained excitement, he waits impatiently for Benvenuto Cellini to knock at his door. He silently surveys the collection of antiquities, busts and medals arranged all around him. His mind is filled with the faces and voices of his friends, many of them dead, a few still alive. His gaze hesitates before alighting on the famous *Mensa Isiaca*, a splendid bronze tablet, also known as the *Tabula Bambina*, representing the goddess Isis accompanied by several other divinities [Figure 3]. Displayed nearby are a gigantic *San Sebastian* by Mantegna, the heads of Julius Cesar, Domitian and Caracalla, a portrait of his brother Carlo, a statue of Amor... Memories of the people and passions of a lifetime. After too many care-filled years at court, in Rome, away from his beloved villa, he is finally free to live as he has always wanted to live: far from the turmoil of court life, amidst his books. He is still unaware that his fate is to be called back to Rome and caught up again in the whirlwind of public life.

When the talented goldsmith finally crosses the threshold of his house and sets to work, Pietro is so eager to see his face take form under the artist's hand that he mistakes a first draft for the final work. In his *Vita*, Benvenuto Cellini notes, with sarcastic sweetness, that Bembo was undoubtedly 'a great man when it came to literature and poetry', but 'with regard to my profession, his Lordship understood nothing of the world'. His assessment seems particularly cruel, considering that Bembo was one of the most distinguished antiquarians and art collectors of his time. At any rate, even though Cellini found it difficult to sculpt a satisfactory portrait of Bembo 'because he wears his beard short, in the Venetian style', the operation was a success, and the artist considered the medal to be 'the most beautiful work I have ever produced'. Bembo secretly gave Cellini three horses in the hope of keeping him in Padua, an example of the discreet generosity of which he was sometimes capable, though in other ways he was quite difficult to please.

A fascinating aspect of that encounter between the famous, humble scholar and the brilliant, but rather conceited, artist is that 'the common father of the Muses', as Bembo was described after his death by the Florentine doctor Benedetto Varchi, seemed intimidated by Cellini (the episode also caught the attention of Giacomo Leopardi, who mentioned it in *Zibaldone* on 5 August 1823). One wonders if the two men — Bembo and Cellini — realised that they were taking part in one of those moments that seem to encapsulate the essence of an era. Their meeting symbolically opposed two faces of the late Renaissance which vied for dominance during that period. The emerging generation included many bold self-promoters intent on shaping their own myth and audience. These artists and writers, many of whom were endowed with brilliant audacity, were keen to explore new paths and substitute new themes, new forms and new genres for the dominant cultural canon, which was still deeply humanistic and rooted in principles such as the imitation and cult of the ancients. The meeting between Cellini and Bembo epitomised the opposition between these two conceptions of culture, which were destined to collide. On the one hand, a creative, visionary, non-conformist genius; on the other, a Humanist scholar who wrote fluently in Latin and Greek, a philologist and antiquarian, an author of poems of exceptional formal purity, albeit modelled on Petrarch and, for the most part, devoid of any real spark of inspiration. Giacomo Leopardi understood the situation well. In *Zibaldone*, on 27 February 1827, he compared the figure of Bembo to a famous pedant of his own time, Antonio Cesari: 'A great deal of reading and study; no genius, be it natural or acquired by art. Never a flash or spark of genius in their writing, never a happy vein. Few or none of our successful authors or books which are still in print have been as lacking in this regard as Bembo and his work.' Leopardi thus consigns both Bembo the author and Bembo the man to the grave: dry, dull, colourless and uninspired. He was wrong, of course, but perhaps he was merely using Bembo to make a point.

Pietro was nothing if not handsome. Tall and gracious, he loved women and they returned the favour, though they had to share his affection with the Muses. He was very attractive, in spite of his injured hand. His eyes were bright and his nose 'rather long and slightly aquiline'. For most of his life he was clean-shaven, but grew a beard in his old age, shortly before being elected as a cardinal. At the time of the meeting with Cellini in 1537, he had been wearing a beard for approximately a year. This detail is not as insignificant as it seems. Indeed, in the first half of the sixteenth century, self-representation — not only through the medium of text but also through the deliberate use of images, which, thanks to the new technology of printing, could be widely reproduced and disseminated via books and engravings — had become a key factor. Pietro Aretino was one of the pioneers of this strategy, and certainly its most skilful practitioner. He was the first to understand that any writer who wished to stake a claim on the literary and social stage must now skilfully manage his image, which was reproduced in paintings, frescoes and medals, and sometimes even on everyday objects. Authors could no longer afford to neglect these methods of self-promotion. To wear or not to wear a beard, or — in Pietro Aretino's case — to dye or not to dye it: such decisions were part of a well thought-out communications strategy. A portrait might take liberties in the way it depicted the individual so as to better target a certain audience, since its purpose was also to convey a set of shared aspirations, convictions and ideals. In a word, a

Fig. 4. Valerio Belli, *Medal of Pietro Bembo*, c. 1532, bronze, diameter 4 cm, Victoria and Albert Museum, London. © Victoria and Albert Museum, London

portrait presumed the existence of a code, which had to be precisely formulated and just as carefully deciphered.

Let us now try to analyse the image of Pietro on Valerio Belli's medal. Bembo is represented in profile, with a high forehead and longish hair falling to his shoulders. The reverse offers a further set of clues: the poet lies next to a river, clearly lost in thought, possibly waiting for inspiration [Figure 4]. The medal was created in 1532 when Bembo was sixty-two. For a viewer accustomed to decoding images such as these, however, the picture clearly harks back to Pietro's youth. A similar scene is described in *De Ætna*, one of Bembo's early dialogues, a conversation between Pietro and his father Bernardo, in which the former recounts his ascent of the Sicilian volcano. The dialogue begins by describing an encounter between the father and the son next to the Piovego River, which flowed through the family's estate of Villa Bozza. In a portrait by Lucas Cranach the Younger painted a few years after the medal was cast, Bembo wears the robe of the Knights of Saint John; he is clean-shaven and has deep-set, piercing eyes and a brooding air. His forehead is high, and his hair sparse and grey. The painting dates from shortly before the famous, large-format portraits of the later years, such as the outstanding Titian, now in Washington, which shows the cardinal with a full beard, striking a sculptural, eloquent pose. He exudes the physical vigour that allowed him, as a young man, to stand up to Giusto's provocation on the Rialto. The portrait was completed in 1539–40, soon after Bembo's election as cardinal: his face is set in an expression of gravity befitting a prince of the Church at a time of worsening religious crisis, which had already caused an unbridgeable rift with the Reformed world to the north of the Alps. The moment was grave, and great hopes were pinned on the elevation to the cardinalship of men such as Bembo and his friends Sadoleto and Gasparo Contarini — well-respected, cultivated humanists who could engage with the Protestant world. Of course, for the most rigorous Catholics on the fringes, the presence of a man like Bembo in the College of Cardinals was highly suspect. Until 1535, he had cohabitated *more uxorio* with Morosina and fathered three children: Lucilio, Elena and Torquato. His love poems were, therefore, far more than an innocent collection of youthful memories, and his passion for classical antiquities was dangerously reminiscent of the pagan atmosphere that suffused Rome during the first two decades of the sixteenth century, a time of many wonderful experiences for Bembo, who was then in his forties. A glimmer of that bygone world and its fascination with classical and pagan culture survived in the seal that Bembo designed for himself after becoming a cardinal: while the seal depicted the baptism of Christ, the handle was in the shape of two winged ephebes.

Curiously, the many known portraits of Bembo, both authenticated and presumed, do not include a medal by Cellini. Maybe it was never finished. However, we know that the design on the reverse represented a crown of myrtle, the sacred tree of Venus, encircling an image of Pegasus, the sacred horse of the Muses, who gave birth to the fountain of Hippocrene. In other words, Pietro was still celebrating poetry and love at the age of sixty-seven. The likely appearance of the image on the reverse can be inferred from another medal, by the sculptor Danese Cattaneo, which shows the mythical horse striking the earth with his hoof to open up the legendary spring. Cattaneo's medal was cast in 1547–48, shortly after Bembo's death. The climate by then had grown much gloomier, following the creation, in 1542, of the Tribunale del Sant'Uffizio, or Inquisition, and the publication, in 1548, by Giovanni Della Casa of his first index of banned books, in the very house in Rome where Cardinal Bembo died. All allusions to love were therefore prudently suppressed. In the same period Cattaneo also sculpted an outstanding bust of the cardinal (now in Basilica del Santo), in which Pietro's beard plays a prominent role. Its profuse tangle of curls, rendered with extraordinary skill, combined with the deeply creased forehead and intense gaze, produce a highly expressive, grave and austere portrait of the master of Italian letters, the most influential writer of the Renaissance.

A lover of poetry, admirer of classical culture, knight of Saint John, stern cardinal: the art of portraiture reveals many facets of Pietro's personality, to which one might add those of skilful orator, man of the world, art collector and lover. But there was one quality that remained a constant throughout every stage of his

Fig. 5. Giulio Bonasone, *Portrait of Pietro Bembo*, 1572, engraving, 23.3 × 17 cm, Metropolitan Museum of Art, New York. Rogers Fund, 1922/www.metmuseum.org

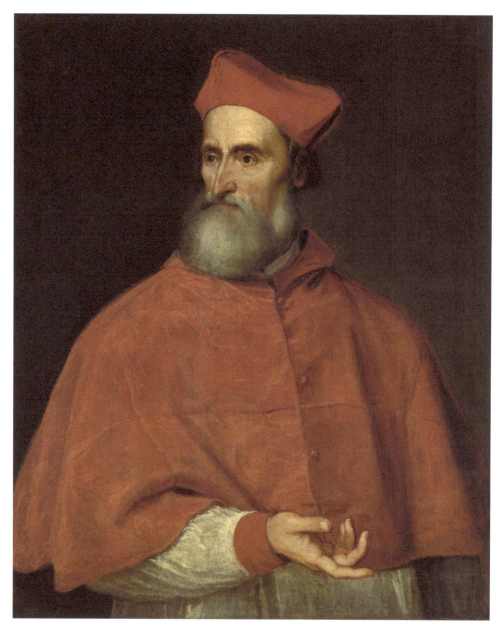

Fig. 6. Titian, *Portrait of Pietro Bembo*, c. 1540, oil on canvas, 94.5 × 76.5 cm, National Gallery of Art, Washington.
Samuel H. Kress Collection/Courtesy National Gallery of Art, Washington

life: his deep devotion to friendship. Though we have yet to truly penetrate the world of Pietro Bembo, even as we stand on the edge, as it were, hesitating to dive into his biography, which spanned the most happy and creative years of the Renaissance as well as its darkest tragedies, and ended at the dawn of a new age — far less free, bold and polyphonic than the one before — a new document comes to our rescue. This short essay, known as the *Leggi della Compagnia degli Amici* [Laws of the Company of Friends], appears under the title *Leggi dell'Amicitia* [Laws of Friendship] in the manuscript thanks to which it is known today (ms. S. 99 sup. Biblioteca Ambrosiana in Milan), as if its true purpose was to lay down the eternal laws of perfect friendship. These few short pages transport us back to Venice in the first years of the sixteenth century, around 1502–03, that is, shortly after Bembo returned there from Ferrara. He was no longer a young man and, though busy with writing his first important work, *Gli Asolani*, he had not yet provided any definitive proof of his talent. Political life had given him no satisfaction yet, despite his father's repeated attempts to advance his career. Fortune had offered him a glimpse of the treasure she held in store for him, but had not yet opened wide her coffers. The temptation to escape into a world of illusion — to seek refuge from the twists and turns of fate, his disappointed hopes, the contemptible plotting and manoeuvring — must have been great.

The *Leggi* were rules designed to govern existing, real-life relationships, but they also had a utopian dimension. For his friends — who were all scholars and patricians like himself — Pietro outlined an ideal republic of letters, in which everything would be held in common, including both what pertained to the soul and what derived from fortune, that is, material possessions. Lying would be forbidden, the enemies of one would be the enemies of all, and bearing arms would be allowed to defend oneself and one's *Amici*, in the name of spiritual brotherhood. The audacity of the young man who was willing to risk his life on the Rialto rather than tolerate an insult echoes in the words of the thirty-year-old author of the *Leggi*.

This short text offers entry into an unusual world. To become a 'friend', one must of course be 'a scholar and man of letters', for to mark every 'joyful' occasion members are required to contribute 'a song or sonnet or other type of poetic composition in Latin'. This ideal world is further characterised by refined tastes in gold work, painting and the courtly fashion for insignia (associations of images and mottos intended to express a certain feeling, intention or character trait; they became very popular in the wake of the French invasion of 1494 and within a few decades had evolved an extensive set of principles). Members were required to carry a small gold medal with a picture of the Graces on one side and the motto 'AMICORUM SODALITATI' on the other, which they pinned to their left arm with a gold chain cast from the same mould 'by the hands of a great master'. Additionally, they would all have their portrait painted 'by the hand of that exceptional painter', with their name and personal insignia inscribed on the back. The *Amici* were expected to share their innermost thoughts as well — their feelings, preoccupations and passions — for nothing in the small republic could remain hidden; even the contents of the heart had to be visible, as if that organ were made of glass.

Yet, the *Amici* were not the stern, ascetic, pedantic men of letters one might assume. On the contrary, when a new member joined the association, existing members were 'required to celebrate for eight consecutive days [...] with every kind of banquet, game and refined discussion' which could decently be organised.

Those precepts encapsulate many of the essential characteristics and rules of the Renaissance, defined by Baldassarre Castiglione shortly afterwards in the *Cortegiano*. They included a love of art, precious objects and classical imagery (the Graces), a taste for insignia, an affinity for friendship and conversation, and a vision of society in which men and women were united by a belief in literature and the noblest values. The most eminent Bembo scholar aptly describes that world as one suffused with 'chivalrous nostalgia' and a courtly, aristocratic experience, somewhat unexpected in such a pragmatic place as Venice. Indeed, the *Leggi* contain no hint of the passion for politics and the mercantile, proto-capitalist culture that characterised the city.

Traces of the *Leggi* appear in a series of sonnets, to which Ludovico Ariosto also contributed. In the first years of the sixteenth century, Pietro Bembo pursued a tortured love for Lucrezia Borgia, wife of the Duke of Ferrara, Alfonso d'Este. In June 1503, he sent her at least three love sonnets. In one of these, *Poi ch'ogni ardir mi circonscrisse Amore*, and in letters from the same period, he began to shape the myth of the 'crystalline heart' ('Would that I had a heart as crystal clear, | that what I hide, nor she can ascertain | without more proof of my least inward pain | would shine for her fair eyes in faith sincere'). The poem is the last in a trio that included *Crin d'oro crespo et d'ambra tersa et pura* (an inventory of Lucrezia's charms) followed by *Moderati desiri, immenso ardore*, which lists the symptoms of lovesickness, including 'to open the heart to two beautiful eyes' and feelings of 'disdain of glass, adamantine faith'. The sonnets for Lucrezia later inspired a sort of poetic joust between two of the *Amici*, Niccolò Tiepolo and Vincenzo Querini; their poems expanded on the list of feminine charms to which Pietro had succumbed. Even Ariosto joined in. The recurrent symbol of the crystal expresses a utopian desire: pure or complete spiritual communion between the lover and his beloved. But among the *Amici* it also marked out a space that was inaccessible to hearts without nobility, a space devoid of any kind of bargaining, compromise and baseness.

That world, however, was as fragile as the crystalline heart that Bembo evoked with such passion. Clearly the need to define 'laws' initially arose in response to the painful realisation that those ideals were in reality quite fragile and precarious, easily slipping through the fingers and disappearing without a trace, as well as the feeling that the profound communion of true friendship had already lost much of its immediacy and spontaneity. As a modern commentator notes, the *Leggi* also expressed nostalgia for a world that had already disappeared. The manuscript contains a number of annotations in a different hand, attributed to Tommaso Giustiniani, one of the *Amici*, which were probably added immediately after the *Leggi* were set down, perhaps following the graceful exchange of sonnets mentioned above. The annotations strike a note of solemn, cautious austerity; they suggest that the *Amici* institute the practice of public confession, during which members would confess their actions over the past year. They also enjoin them to forgo marriage, abstain from carnal pleasures, and avoid eating meat and drinking wine. The religious preoccupations underlying these annotations prompted their author, the priest and future hermit Tommaso Giustiniani, to retire soon afterwards to the hermitage of Camaldoli. They also inspired him to write, in collaboration with Vincenzo Querini, a *Libellum ad Leonem X* (1513), containing a list of suggestions for reforming the Church, which was published shortly before the violent eruption of the Lutheran Reformation. The *Leggi* thus encapsulated a bygone and probably idealised moment in time, since, in reality, most of the *Amici* either went on to a career in public service or chose a more austere, religious path or, like Pietro, simply left the city. New preoccupations and opportunities loomed on the horizon. But what impelled Pietro to take the next step?

CHAPTER 2

'To rise above the common mud': The Dream of Literature

In July 1478, the Venetian ambassador Bernardo Bembo arrived in Florence, where he remained until May 1480. His young son Pietro came with him. It was a volatile time; in April, the Pazzi, a family of bankers who were in direct competition with the Medici, conspired to challenge the supremacy of their rivals. Although Florence was officially a republic, in actual fact it was governed by Lorenzo il Magnifico in the manner of a sovereign. The Pazzi planned to assassinate him and his brother Giuliano. On Sunday 26 April 1478, the two brothers were attacked during Mass in the Duomo. Lorenzo survived, but Giuliano succumbed after suffering nineteen dagger wounds at the hands of his assailants. The plot was violently repressed, in large part by the people of Florence themselves. The Pazzi had assumed incorrectly that their fellow citizens would reject the despotism of the Medici, when in fact the Florentines were faithful to their rulers.

It was Bernardo's second mission to Florence, and he found himself in a very delicate position. After the Pazzi conspiracy — behind which there loomed the *longa manus* of Pope Sixtus IV, who had his sights set on Florence's possessions, and of his armed hand, Federico da Montefeltro — war was declared. The pope, with Ferrante d'Aragon, King of Naples, and Federico da Montefeltro, led a campaign of sieges and surprise attacks. Florence's allies, Venice and the duchy of Milan, were unwilling to intervene, for various reasons. The assassination of Duke Galeazzo Maria Sforza in 1476 had created a power vacuum in Milan, as his heir Gian Galeazzo was only seven years old. The regency fell to the boy's mother, Bona, assisted by Chancellor Cicco Simonetta. Venice, with characteristic prudence, played for time, with the aim of assessing the forces in play. Florence was not a military power and relied on mercenaries, a notoriously unmanageable lot. By contrast, the pope's troops were led by one of the most fearsome generals in the land, the experienced and wily 'Light of Italy,' one-eyed Federico da Montefeltro. Bernardo thus had to perform a difficult balancing act: as a diplomat, his aim was to gain time and delay Venetian involvement, while his old friend Lorenzo, whose kingdom was under threat, pressed him for help. The peace that had prevailed since 1454 was soon to end.

The young Pietro was thus immersed from a young age in a roiling cauldron of alliances, betrayals and conspiracies. However, that period of murderous conflict was merely a dark spot on an otherwise uniquely brilliant era in cultural history. Florence in the 1470s and 1480s was the cradle of Italian civilisation. The arts, literature and philology — influenced by the rediscovery of the classical authors of antiquity — flourished with unequalled vigour. Lorenzo il Magnifico, Marsilio Ficino and Angelo Poliziano were the main sponsors of a cultural policy centred on the Neoplatonic notion of love. The love poetry developed by the Neoplatonists conveyed philosophical and allegorical values, and presented love as a privileged way to understand the divine and communicate with it. Its followers also cultivated an appreciation of the joys and beauty of life, made all the keener by an awareness of its fragility. In parallel with this decidedly noble style, there also emerged a more playful style of poetry, celebrating the pleasures of love. The complex ideas developed within Lorenzo's circle of friends were repeated and reflected, as in a mirror, through masques, jousts, parades and allegories, thus fostering their widespread diffusion. Pietro, though very young at the time, had the opportunity to familiarise himself with this extraordinary atmosphere. He met Lorenzo de' Medici, who gave him a small and beautiful white horse, and frequented intellectuals of a calibre far superior to his former tutors, including Giovanni Alessandro Urticio, and probably Giovanni Aurelio Augurelli, an outstanding scholar with very broad interests and an admirer of Petrarch.

Given Pietro's young age, it is impossible to know if his ties to the Medici family, which he maintained until middle age, date from that period, but it seems fairly certain that the connection came neither through Giulio de' Medici, future Pope Clement VII, who was born in 1478, nor Lorenzo's son Giovanni, later Pope Leo X, born in December 1475 and barely three years old at the time. There is no record of the impression that Angelo Poliziano made on Pietro; despite the latter's precocity, he was probably too young to fully understand the brilliant philologist. However, we know that Bernardo Bembo was in regular contact with Poliziano, as well as Marsilio Ficino and many others in Lorenzo il Magnifico's circle. An exceptional document from that period provides a first, indirect sign of Pietro's activity as a poet, in the form of a sonnet dedicated to him. The poem, which praises a sonnet composed by the nine-year-old Pietro, appears in a manuscript in the Florence State Archive (ms. Carte Strozziane, s. II, CXXXV), containing recollections of the Tedaldi family and a small collection of poems. Intriguingly, in addition to praising of Pietro as a 'dicitor perfetto', it predicts that he 'will soon aspire to emulate Petrarch' and, inspired by his father's example, become a 'great monarch' of letters, especially if he continues to study philosophy. The poem also notes the boy's unusually precocious formal skill, his admiration for Petrarch and his already marked interest in philosophy. The author of the poem is unknown, but it is frequently attributed to Giovanni Aurelio Augurelli; it seems likely that he became Pietro's tutor, due to his longstanding friendship with Bernardo. Augurelli was certainly proud of his pupil, as indicated by the laudatory poem *Ad musam in Petri Bembi P. Veneti laudem* (To the Muse, in Praise of Pietro Bembo, Patrician of Venice), included in the second volume of his *Carminum libri*.

Intellectual precocity and a love for Petrarch are the hallmarks of a second text, lovingly recorded by Bernardo in his own hand. It is an epigram in Latin, which praises Petrarch and mocks a man named Matteo Gerardo for his awkwardness in declaiming verse. Bernardo recorded in a note that the poem was written by 'Petrus meus' ('my Pietro') in 1484 as they were travelling together on horseback to Rome on a diplomatic mission to Pope Innocent VIII. The embassy to Rome actually took place a year later; Bernardo may have mistaken the dates when transcribing the epigram onto the endpapers of one of his favourite manuscripts (which contained Seneca's *Epistolæ ad Lucilium*, Eton College, ms. 135).

Not much is known about Pietro's early childhood and education, as the preceding discussion clearly indicates. He next appears in the documentary records — insofar as his intellectual development is concerned — at the age of twenty-one. He was by then immersed in his studies and enjoyed the great privilege of working with the remarkable Poliziano [Figure 7]. Poliziano spent the summer of 1491 travelling through northern Italy with Giovanni Pico della Mirandola searching for manuscripts of ancient authors. He was received on his arrival in Venice by his old friend Bernardo Bembo. The great philologist was no doubt overjoyed at the sight of a manuscript Pietro presented to him: a late fourth- or early fifth-century copy of the *Comedies* of Terence (ms. Vat Lat. 3226 in the Vatican Apostolic Library). Rapidly scanning the text, which was written in the ancient script, that is, entirely in capitals, his expert eye immediately noted important textual variations with known versions, many of which were crucial for resolving incomplete or altered passages. He immediately sent out to a bookseller for a copy of the *Comedies* published in 1475 in order to note the textual variants he spotted in its margins. He started work on 23 June; young Pietro, whom he described in a note as a 'studiosus litterarum adolescens', provided valuable help. Not content with assisting the master, Pietro procured a copy of the published *Comedies* for himself, in which he recorded all the variants observed by Poliziano as well as his own observations (both copies have survived: Poliziano's is now in the Biblioteca Nazionale Centrale, and Pietro's duplication of the Florentine philologist's work in the Veneranda Biblioteca Ambrosiana of Milan).

Pietro's friend Girolamo Savorgnan was also a witness to that endeavour; Poliziano meticulously recorded his name in his copy of Terence, although he probably did not take part in the project. Savorgnan, who died in 1529, was four years older than Pietro, and was destined for a brilliant career as a military leader, defeating several attacks by the German army against Cadore, on the outer reaches of the Venetian Republic. Immediately after he died, Bembo praised Savorgnan as 'wise', 'good', and a man of 'great courage' in a sonnet in honour of another recently deceased friend, Andrea Navagero (*Navagier mio, ch'a terra strana vòlto*). And much earlier, possibly in 1491, certainly before May 1492, Bembo dedicated his first important work, *Sogno*, a poem of 193 hendecasyllables in linked tercets (the metre of Dante's *Divina Commedia* and Petrarch's *Trionfi*) to Savorgnan. An introductory letter addressed to Savorgnan describes this work as the fruit of many restless nights, 'which fate, as you well know, has decreed shall be my lot from now on.' We do not know what was disturbing Bembo's sleep: an unhappy love perhaps (sonnets from that period allude to a recently ended affair), worries regarding his studies, or the torments of a young man's yearning for glory? Be that as it may, he presented the

Fig. 7. Domenico Ghirlandaio, *Scenes from the Life of St Francis: Confirmation of the Franciscan Rule by Pope Honorius III*, c. 1482–85, fresco, Sassetti Chapel, basilica of Santa Trinita, Florence (detail: Angelo Poliziano). © 2015. Photo Scala, Florence

poem, with great modesty and 'not [...] without blushing', as a 'small and first gift.' As its title indicates, the *Sogno* describes an allegorical vision that came to Pietro in a dream. Pietro and Girolamo are in a cold cave, which is filled with flowers and at the mouth of which they can glimpse a shaft of sunlight. Pietro stands, leaning against a rock, while his friend sits on the grass. Both are naked. They are deep in conversation when a simply dressed woman with a virtuous air approaches them. In a long speech, she exhorts them to abandon their vague pastimes, avoid vanity and devote themselves instead to studying and cultivating knowledge. Life is short, she says, and time flies swiftly; one must therefore use it wisely to perform virtuous actions. In words that admit no reply, she enjoins Pietro and Girolamo to forsake the company of men who live in a state close to that of animals, and to 'rise above the common mud'. The accusation of corruption levelled against their contemporaries is reinforced by comparison with the virtues of the ancient Romans, who espoused a simple lifestyle focusing on the common good. Pietro is troubled by the words of this mysterious apparition; he worries that he is unworthy. But the woman, who 'saw my thoughts through my forehead, like a bright bud shining under glass or next to a spring', reassures him graciously and ends her speech by asking Girolamo to take good care of young Pietro, as he will soon have to follow in his footsteps.

Who is the mysterious woman? According to some she represents Philosophy; for others, Philology. In either case, she conveys a marked taste for allegorical and oneiric visions, which is perfectly illustrated by the *Hypnerotomachia Poliphili*, an allegorical and philosophical novel considered by many to be the most significant printed work of the Renaissance. Written by the mysterious Francesco Colonna, it was published by Aldo Manuzio in 1499. Notice the date: Bembo's *Sogno* probably appeared in 1498. Incidentally, Pietro sent a copy of his book as a gift to Alberto Pio, Lord of Carpi, a nephew of Giovanni Pico della Mirandola, who happened to be a student of Aldo Manuzio. The *Sogno* is thus situated at a crossroads between Pietro's past and future. The connection to his past is made apparent by clear indications of his deep familiarity with the Florentine philosophers and their ideas (which inspired the themes of the transience of life and the exaltation of human nature and its capacity for reason, as well as the poem's allegorical nature). Conversely, the obvious influence of Dante and Petrarch in the poetic scheme, as well as that of Aldo Manuzio, visible throughout the book, foreshadow Pietro's future: he would later make his unforgettable début on the literary scene thanks to those three names.

It would be false to assume that the decision to become a writer was an easy one for Pietro. On the contrary, to be allowed to devote his life to scholarship he first had to overcome the objections of his mother and father. According to Monsignor Giovanni Della Casa, it was only after 'much arguing by the son and much admonishing and reprimanding by his father and his mother, Elena Marcello' that Pietro was finally released from the obligation of serving 'at the mercy of the people and the ignorant multitude'. For the scion of such an ancient and prominent patrician family to renounce Venetian political life was not an obvious choice, even in the eyes of a man of such broad and versatile culture as Bernardo. The elder Bembo cultivated a deep interest in literature and art. His collection included, among others, a diptych of John the Baptist and Saint Veronica by Hans Memling (a portrait by Memling in the Koninklijk Museum, Antwerp, is thought to represent Bernardo Bembo). He is also believed to have commissioned Leonardo da Vinci's famous portrait of Ginevra de' Benci. Moreover, he was close to Pietro and Tullio Lombardo, two famous sculptors whom he commissioned to restore Dante's tomb when he was *podestà* of Ravenna. At his request, they designed two monumental columns modelled after those in the Piazzetta in Venice, a clear sign of Bernardo's enduring interest in architecture. He also purchased a manuscript of *De re ædificatoria* by Leon Battista Alberti, with an attached fascicle of autograph corrections (Eton College, ms. 128). In addition to the above-mentioned artists, his circle of friends included the mathematician Luca Pacioli; Fra Giocondo, the author of a seminal edition of Vitruvius's *De architectura*, printed in 1511; and the great copyist and miniaturist Bartolomeo Sanvito.

Despite the breadth of his interests — from agriculture to urbanism and antiquities — Bernardo was first and foremost an outstanding politician. His crowning achievement was his election to the Council of Ten, the highest governing body of the Republic of Venice. Bernardo wanted Pietro to follow in his footsteps. This was merely what was expected of any young Venetian nobleman: to serve his country by entering the judiciary or the government, possibly the army. But Pietro's political career was a long series of fiascos. On 30 July 1499, he applied for the position of *pagator in campo*. Rejected. On 19 December 1500, he was in the running for an ambassadorship to Hungary. Rejected. On 30 March 1501, he put in for a diplomatic mission to Portugal. Rejected. On 8 March 1504, he applied to become ambassador to France. Rejected. Ten days later, on 18 March, he was a candidate for an embassy to Germany and Spain. Rejected. On 16 December, he petitioned for an embassy to Burgundy. Rejected again. A few months later, Bernardo, still trying to secure a good position for his son, who was overly inclined to courting women and writing poetry, submitted Pietro's name for embassies to the King of France and the Emperor respectively (1 and 14 June 1505). No need to specify the outcome. But Bernardo was stubborn and, much to his credit, spared no effort. Aware that further diplomatic missions were being planned, namely to the King of Spain and to Naples (4 September and 7 October 1505), he persisted. This time, he was sure Pietro would be chosen. But he was disappointed. The only option now open to Pietro was to leave Venice to seek employment at one of the many Italian courts. However, that meant renouncing his political rights as a Venetian patrician. It was an agonising choice. This context goes a long way toward explaining his famous complaint in a letter to his friend Giovanni Battista Ramusio, following the publication of a pirated copy of his *Prose della volgar lingua*: 'I have said it before, and I feel it is true: everywhere I have gone in the world I have received honours, friendship and advantages, whereas in my homeland I have received nothing but shame, indifference and complications.'

Bembo did not make peace with the Republic until 1530, when he was hired to finish the history of Venice begun by his friend Andrea Navagero. The recognition was a belated one, however. The history attests to the central role played by his youthful ambitions. Fate, he wrote, had decreed that the price for obtaining this prestigious commission was the death of his friend Andrea. In the tranquil setting of his house in Padua — 'my father's little house' — he thus began a conversation with his family ghosts and the dreams of his youth. The present was marred by sickness (Bembo had only recently 'recovered [his] health after [...] his Roman labours') and overshadowed by the arduous task of recording more than fifty years of Venice's convulsive history, from 1486, where his predecessor Marco Antonio Sabellico had broken off (Navagero, though richly paid, had apparently never written a single line), to the present, that is, 1530 (though, in fact, Bembo would only get as far as 1513). Bembo compounded the burden by writing the *Historia vinitiana* in Latin and then translating it into the vernacular, between 1544 and 1546. Yet despite the huge amount of work it involved, he was determined to 'spare no effort to satisfy their [i.e. his fellow citizen's] aspirations'. And so Pietro finally made peace with Venice.

But this digression has transported us unawares to the end of Pietro's story. Let us now step back in time to the period immediately after the publication of the *Sogno*. Pietro decided it was time to complete his education. Looking back at the road already travelled, he saw a limited poetic *oeuvre*: fewer than a dozen poems, written between 1492 and 1493. They are known today thanks to a manuscript in the Bibliothèque Nationale de Paris (Ital. 1543), originally copied in Milan, probably at the request of Gasparo Visconti, a famous poet of the time. Pietro's verses were likely circulated in Milan by Galeazzo Facino, a poet, scholar of Greek, philosopher and traveller from Padua, who was connected to the Milanese court between 1489 and 1490. Facino maintained ties with prominent humanists, such as Ermolao Barbaro and Girolamo Donà, who were friends of Bernardo; it is not surprising, therefore, to find him acting as a kind of sponsor for the promising young poet. Pietro wrote a sonnet in his honour, *Se le sorelle, che, nascendo, prima* (which he later recycled, somewhat cavalierly, for his friend Federico Fregoso). In addition to his indisputable talent as a poet, Pietro was fluent in Latin and well-versed in fourteenth-century poetry, philology and philosophy. But to be considered truly accomplished as a Humanist he needed to learn Greek, too. There was a Greek master in Messina who was considered to be the best in his field: his name was Costantino Lascaris. The decision was quickly taken, and Pietro set sail for Sicily to study under the great scholar.

Lascaris was one of a large number of Greeks who arrived in Italy after the fall of the Byzantine Empire in 1453. He taught for several years in Milan, at the court of Francesco Sforza, and later in Rome and Naples. He benefited from the protection of the powerful and highly cultivated Cardinal Bessarione, who tirelessly campaigned to avert the impending Ottoman invasion and negotiated at length with the most powerful men in the land, from Pope Pius II to Federico da Montefeltro, with the aim of organising a crusade. In 1472, Pope Sixtus IV sent Bessarione to meet Louis XI of France and argue the case for a military expedition to restore the Byzantine Empire. The expedition never set out, but Bessarione managed to save a great number of Greek books, which were the core of his extensive and highly valuable library. For a cultivated Venetian such as Bembo, the name of Cardinal Bessarione must have exerted an irresistible fascination. In 1468, the cardinal donated 746 manuscripts to the city of Venice — another 250 were added after his death — which formed the first nucleus of the Biblioteca Marciana. In other words, Lascaris was a worthy heir to an ancient and very noble tradition.

In May 1492, twenty years after the death of Cardinal Bessarione, Pietro left for Messina. He stopped along the way in Naples. There, it seems likely that he met the great Humanist Giovanni Pontano, who dedicated the seventh volume of his *De rebus cœlestibus* to him. In the following years, Pietro was in regular contact with Neapolitan humanists, especially Jacopo Sannazaro, the author of *Arcadia* and an important collection of *Rime*, published posthumously in 1530, at the same time as Pietro's. An accomplished Latin poet, as attested by his sacred poem *De Partu Virginis*, Sannazaro corresponded with Pietro for many years. When he died, Pietro dedicated a Latin epigram to him. Moreover, a portrait of Sannazaro appears among the artworks that Pietro collected in his house in Padua.

As his travel and study companion, Pietro chose a contemporary, Angelo Gabriel. Equipped with a solid humanistic education, Gabriel was destined to become a prototypical Venetian patrician, entirely devoted to the Republic, a career path that Bembo was neither able nor willing to follow. After Messina, Angelo studied in Padua, where he came into contact with a group of cultivated intellectuals that gravitated around Aldo Manuzio and his Academy. His meagre literary production — in Latin only — glorified the central events and protagonists of political life in the Serenissima: the death of a doge or celebrations organised for the arrival of a monarch, for instance. Angelo was first and foremost a faithful servant of the Republic: he fought in many of the wars in which Venice was embroiled during the first decades of the century and held public offices, including that of *avogador di comun*. He died in 1533.

De Ætna [Figure 8], the book Pietro completed after returning to Venice, describes those two years in Messina as the happiest of his life. This ambitious work, in the form of a dialogue between Pietro and his father, interweaves scientific explanations of volcanic activity, the genesis of lava rocks and the origins of the wind, with archaeological and antiquarian quotations, and learned commentaries. Yet *De Ætna* was far more than a youthful literary exercise. Produced by Aldo Manuzio in 1496, this elegant book marks the first appearance of roman type. Its legible, Humanist letter-forms were revived in 1929 as a font called Bembo, and are widely used in book design even today: this biography, for example, is typeset in Bembo. The publication of *De Ætna* is therefore a small milestone in the history of typography, and confirms Bembo's remarkable foresight concerning the development of the emerging publishing industry.

The roman typeface used in *De Ætna* was created by Manuzio's celebrated punch-cutter Francesco Griffo, who would later also invent the cursive font known as italic. Griffo's roman font was probably inspired by the calligraphy of Bartolomeo Sanvito, itself based on the monumental style of the imperial period. Additionally, *De Ætna* was the first book to use modern punctuation marks (commas, semicolons, quotation marks) and accents. It was thus far more than a scholastic exercise by a young nobleman — in fact Pietro no longer qualified as young — who had offered only limited proof of his talent until then. Rather, it represented the first stage of

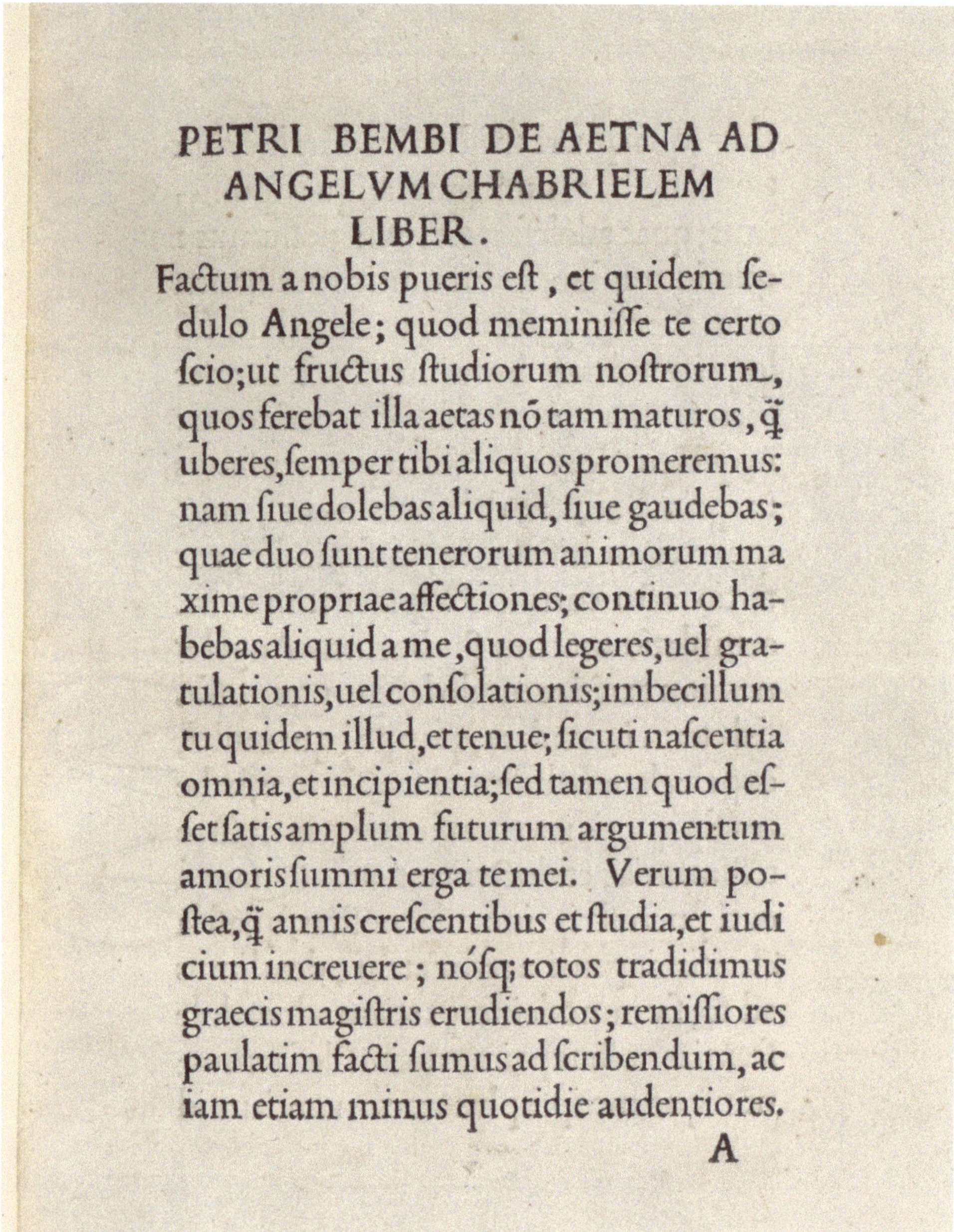

PETRI BEMBI DE AETNA AD ANGELVM CHABRIELEM LIBER.

Factum a nobis pueris est, et quidem sedulo Angele; quod meminisse te certo scio;ut fructus studiorum nostrorum, quos ferebat illa aetas nõ tam maturos, q̃ uberes, semper tibi aliquos promeremus: nam siue dolebas aliquid, siue gaudebas; quae duo sunt tenerorum animorum maxime propriae affectiones; continuo habebas aliquid a me, quod legeres, uel gratulationis, uel consolationis; imbecillum tu quidem illud, et tenue; sicuti nascentia omnia, et incipientia; sed tamen quod esset satis amplum futurum argumentum amoris summi erga te mei. Verum postea, q̃ annis crescentibus et studia, et iudicium increuere; nósq; totos tradidimus graecis magistris erudiendos; remissiores paulatim facti sumus ad scribendum, ac iam etiam minus quotidie audentiores.

A

Fig. 8. Pietro Bembo, *Petri Bembi De Ætna ad Angelum Chabrielem liber,* Impressus Venetiis, in ædibus Aldi Romani mense februario MVD, c. Air, Cambridge University Library. Reproduced by the kind permission of the Syndics of Cambridge University Library (4.B.3.134 [4580])

a cultural project initiated by an elite and was closely connected to the publication in 1476, in Milan, also by Aldo Manuzio, of Lascaris's Greek grammar, *Erotemata*, the first book printed entirely in Greek. In the preface to the revised edition of his grammar, Aldo boasted of the many improvements made to this new version, which was fully revised and corrected by Lascaris. It incorporated five hundred changes, including 'a few deletions [...], many corrections and untold additions'. Moreover, its publication was made possible by two 'patritii Veneti', Bembo and Gabriel; Aldo emphasised their aristocratic status, which in Bembo's case served to highlight the continuity with the work of other scions of noble families who had devoted themselves to the study of Greek, especially Girolamo Donà and Ermolao Barbaro. Those two great humanists, born in the mid-1450s, loyally served the Republic and carried out many missions on its behalf. Pietro, then in his late twenties, had spent the two previous years immersed in study. Yet he was still expected eventually to follow in the footsteps of his famous forebears by devoting himself to civic life and serving the Republic of Venice.

De Ætna reflects a crucial moment: the choice between *negotia* and *otia*, that is, an active life versus a life devoted to literature. This is the central theme of the discussion which the book's two protagonists engage in after the son discovers his father seated by the river flowing through the fields of their beautiful villa in Noniano, near Padua, seemingly lost in thought. For the father, the villa has always represented a peaceful retreat from the cares and tumult of political life; he goes there to reflect and regain his balance. However, this time he appears to his son to be deeply troubled. Neither the bright fields nor the serried ranks of poplars, clear water and soothing murmur of the river can distract him from the heavy cares of government. But this does not seem to worry him. On the contrary, he explains to Pietro, he has no desire to be free of worry about the Republic, nor would he ever want it to be so. Since he was a young man, his entire life has been directed toward a single purpose, which is the pole star of his every action: to prepare himself to answer the call of the fatherland and serve it loyally. The Republic in turn has entrusted him with many prestigious missions and important embassies, from which he has gained experience, wisdom and authority. In Bernardo's view, for Pietro to leave his homeland would be tantamount to abandoning his father in his old age. Family ties and national allegiance thus combine in a single attribute: that of patrician of Venice.

At the age of twenty-five, Pietro was a cultivated Humanist who could write exquisitely in the most refined Latin and had a perfect mastery of Greek, of which his father knew only a little. As Bernardo wrote to Pietro de' Medici on 25 May 1493, Pietro, after completing a translation of Gorgias's *Encomium* on the abduction of Helen, dedicated to the viceroy of Sicily, seemed ready to become 'grecolo tuto'. The real question, however, was how he should put his erudition to use and combine it with civic ideals. Pietro, for his part, had some very clear ideas on the question.

After returning to Venice, he wrote an Oration (*Oratio pro litteris græcis*), which he seems to still have hoped to publish in 1509. In it, he advocated the study of Greek and Hellenistic civilisation, which had come under threat in Italy, too, since the fall of the Byzantine Empire. Between 1492 and 1494, a whole generation of Greek scholars and passionate amateurs had passed away. This must have affected Pietro deeply; in January 1505, in a letter to his friend Filippo Beroaldo, he mentioned the names of Pico, Poliziano, Pontano, Pomponio Leto and Ermolao. Was any city in a better position than Venice to save the great legacy of Greek civilisation, so much of which had already disappeared? The Republic was more prosperous and peaceful, and owned more books, than any other city in the world; its soldiers and merchants controlled the main islands and cities of Greece; Venetian galleys sailed daily to Corfu, Crete and Rhodes. Why not seize this opportunity to save and protect a priceless legacy? Bembo knew that the political class he was addressing was primarily motivated by practical concerns. He therefore argued that Greek culture was the foundation of philosophy, which was indispensable for governing a country; of logic, which was fundamental to reasoning; and of rhetoric and etymologies, which were essential for writing persuasive speeches. Despite its brilliance, his attempt to reconcile *studia humanitatis* and civic duty fell on deaf ears. Bernardo's view of scholarship as a pleasant interlude between political negotiations was incompatible with Pietro's project. The son had already shown that he understood the huge potential of typography and, with the *Sogno* and *De Ætna*, had positioned himself at centre stage in the role of a pure intellectual.

He still needed to choose, and choose decisively, for the political situation was growing more alarming by the day. September 1494 brought the death of Pietro's old friend Poliziano and the young prodigy Pico della Mirandola, as well as a disastrous new development: the invasion of Italy by the troops of Charles VIII of France, which signalled the beginning of a period of wars, alliances and betrayals. Skilfully exploiting dynastic rivalries among the ruling families of Italy, the French king invaded the peninsula in a bid to conquer the kingdom of Naples, which was ruled at the time by the house of Aragon, by virtue of their status as distant descendants of the Anjou dynasty. He benefited from the help of Ludovico Sforza (Ludovico il Moro), who was intent on supplanting the reigning duke, Gian Galeazzo Sforza, husband of Isabella d'Aragon. Charles VIII advanced as far as Florence, where Piero di Lorenzo de' Medici, originally an ally of the King of Naples, Alfonso II d'Aragon, wavered at first. He eventually sided with the French and gave them control of Pisa, Livorno and a string of fortresses. The people of Florence responded by driving out the Medici and choosing the Dominican monk Girolamo Savonarola as their ruler.

After years of peace and economic, artistic and intellectual prosperity, war sounded a terrible wakeup call for Italy. In the opening pages of his *Storia d'Italia*, the Florentine historian Francesco Guicciardini provided a wonderful description of this sudden transformation:

> It is obvious that ever since the Roman Empire, more than a thousand years ago, weakened mainly by the corruption of its ancient customs, began to decline from that peak which it had achieved as a result of marvelous skill and fortune, Italy had never enjoyed such prosperity or known so favourable a situation as that in which it found itself so securely at rest in the year of our Christian salvation, 1490, and the years immediately before and after. The greatest peace and tranquillity reigned everywhere; the land under cultivation no less in the

most mountainous and arid regions than in the most fertile plains and areas; dominated by no power other than her own, not only did Italy abound in inhabitants, merchandise and riches, but she was also highly renowned for the magnificence of many princes, for the splendor of so many most noble and beautiful cities, as the seat and majesty of religion, and flourishing with men most skilful in the administration of public affairs and most nobly talented in all disciplines and distinguished and industrious in all the arts.

In a little under thirty years, between 1494 and the sack of Rome in May 1527, all that was wiped out. To enter political life at such a time must have appeared increasingly risky to Pietro. By contrast, literature may have seemed like a much safer option. It was to that peaceful haven, therefore, that he turned his ship: he decided to continue his studies in philosophy, and possibly law as well, at the school of the famous scholar Niccolò Leonico Tomeo in Padua. The latter, around forty at the time (he was born in 1456), taught some the greatest minds of the day, including Pietro. He was held in high esteem by Erasmus of Rotterdam, whose students included the future Cardinal Reginald Pole, and corresponded with both Thomas More and the Frenchman Christophe de Longueil, whose premature death Bembo mourned in an epitaph in elegiac verse. Bembo struck up a friendship with Leonico that was far deeper than usual for a disciple and master, and wrote a sonnet commemorating his death (*Leonico, che 'n terra al ver sí spesso*) as well as the Latin inscription on his tomb in the church of San Francesco in Padua.

Torn between politics and literature, Pietro could nevertheless count on the support of a solid private entourage. One figure in particular stands out: a young man named Cola Bruno, who had followed him from Messina. Born in 1480, he studied, like Pietro, under Lascaris. Pietro and Cola immediately became fast friends, and the friendship continued until the latter's death, in 1542. Cola was in charge of Pietro's papers, editing his writings — Pietro had complete confidence in his competence as a man of letters — and supervising their publication. He also managed the household in Padua and, later, the education of two of Pietro's children, Elena and Torquato. This learned and gentle man was as generous as he was modest. He was on good terms with most of Bembo's friends and therefore connected to some of the most influential writers of the age; he became especially close to Monsignor Ludovico Beccadelli, Pietro's biographer. He was highly cultivated, fluent in Latin and Greek, and his poetry could rival that of many of his contemporaries. He was particularly fond of suggesting revisions to Pietro. The latter compensated him monetarily but also by trusting him unconditionally. In his first will, dated 25 November 1535, Bembo wrote:

> I pray Messer Cola never to leave my household, but to remain with my children for the rest of his years, as he has been with me for the better part of his life. I bequeath him my writings and compositions in Latin, Greek and the vernacular, and leave him at liberty to publish whatever he considers fit to print, requesting only that he makes sure it is printed faithfully and without error.

Forty years earlier, however, all was still to be decided, all seemed doubtful. Only a decisive event could indicate the path that Pietro should take.

CHAPTER 3

This Sacred Lead

In that time of great doubt, fate finally offered Pietro a golden opportunity. In 1497, his father was sent to Ferrara on several prestigious political missions, and decided to take his son with him, as he had done in 1489 to Florence and Bergamo. Bernardo remained there only until 1499, but Pietro stayed on in Ferrara, where he had an opportunity to study under the philosopher, doctor and naturalist Niccolò da Lonigo, who went by the Latin name 'Leoniceno'. The aged professor — he was born in 1428 — was held in high esteem by Erasmus, and was a close associate of Aldo Manuzio, with whom he travelled in search of manuscripts of the ancient authors (in particular Aristotle and Galen; they collaborated on the first edition of Aristotle in Greek, published between 1495 and 1498, which played a crucial role in restoring the philosopher's original texts). Manuzio published Leoniceno's works, including a 1497 treatise on syphilis *De epidemia quam Itali morbum Gallicum vocant* [On the Epidemic that the Italians Call the French Disease]. This subject was a highly topical, since the troops of Charles VIII had contributed significantly to the spread of the disease in Italy (hence its name). Leoniceno was also an outstanding philologist, as he proved by correcting Pliny's *Historia naturalis*, and publishing a book on the subject in 1492, which he dedicated to Ermolao Barbaro.

Pietro interrupted his stay in Ferrara between late 1499 and 1501, while he applied for several positions, for which he was invariably rejected. Nevertheless, he returned home and strived to comply with his father's expectations. It seemed like a good time to do so: on 15 April 1499, Venice, though at first hostile to the French, signed the agreement of Blois. The Serenissima detected an opportunity to take the Duchy of Milan in a pincer movement, with the French attacking from the west and the Venetian army preparing for battle on the east.

Nothing could distract Pietro from his literary vocation, however; his stay in Ferrara merely confirmed this. The city was a vibrant centre of culture. From the early fifteenth century, Ferrara emerged as one of the most refined courts in Europe, under the leadership of Niccolò III and Leonello, followed by Ercole d'Este, who occupied the throne when Pietro first arrived. Ferrara's exceptional position in the already exceptional context of the Italian cultural landscape of the period was due to the presence of humanists such as Leon Battista Alberti and Guarino Guarini, as well as a famous school of miniaturists; the invitations extended to the great Flemish musicians in vogue at the time; the broad dissemination of topics inspired by Arthurian chivalric tradition and the love poetry of the troubadours; and the influence of artists such as Pisanello and Cosmè Tura, who, along with Pellegrino Prisciani, designed the famous cycle of astrological frescos in Palazzo Schifanoia, executed by Francesco del Cossa and Ercole de' Roberti between 1468 and 1470 to celebrate the accession of Duke Borso d'Este. The city was also a centre of mannerist poetry and epistolary literature, the most famous of which were composed by the Ferraran poet Antonio Tebaldeo; of theatre, which was a veritable passion in Ferrara, with regular performances of the plays of Plautus and local playwrights; of chivalric literature, which, long before the publication of *Orlando Furioso* by Ariosto, another Ferraran, included masterpieces such as *L'inamoramento de Orlando* by the graceful poet Count Matteo Maria Boiardo; and of a highly sophisticated Latin poetry, illustrated by two authors, the father and son Tito Vespasiano and Ercole Strozzi, who became firm friends with Pietro. This cultural efflorescence could only captivate Pietro. It must have seemed like a completely different world from Venice and the constant manoeuvring, mercantile culture and the civic Humanism it imposed on its native sons.

Great plans were taking shape in Pietro's mind. He had been thinking of writing a book on love for some time. On 11 December 1497, he informed his friend Trifon Gabriele in a letter that he was now spending most of the hours after daybreak writing *Gli Asolani*, which suggests that his close friends were already aware of the project. A few years later, Pietro's efforts resulted in his first real success as an author, the equivalent of a best-seller. Had this dialogue about the nature of love been inspired by an unhappy love affair? The answer is probably yes. It had been a particularly intense and lasting love that shook him to his core and lingered even after he became involved with another woman. But more about that later.

During the nearly five years Bembo spent in Ferrara, two dominant inclinations seem to have to have emerged and become closely intertwined in his mind: on the one hand, a boundless fascination with the topic of love, whose many turbulent, sensual, tormented and delicate manifestations he determined to research, analyse and put into practice; on the other, a devouring passion for literature, guided and buttressed by the rigorous philological principles instilled in the course of his humanistic education. The Ferraran years, which were interrupted by several trips back to Venice, as mentioned earlier, and two to Rome in May 1502 and March 1505 (on the way back, he visited the most brilliant Italian courts of the day), were an important period: he published two seminal editions of Petrarch and Dante, as well as *Gli Asolani*, and cultivated a passionate and tormented relationship with Lucrezia Borgia.

After so many intense experiences, Pietro needed a change of scene. He made a short trip to Venice, travelled down the Adriatic coast and crossed the Montefeltro hills to Urbino, where he arrived in 1506. He was immediately welcomed as a figure of great authority, a prince of letters, the prophet of a new and elegant style of literature, an arbiter on all questions of love.

It is interest to note that he initially gained notoriety due to his role as the editor of two books in the vernacular. He thus attained literary supremacy through an exacting philological exercise consisting in the long and arduous task of transcribing and comparing different versions of Dante and Petrarch. In this area as well, Bembo was a pioneer: he was the first to apply philology to the vernacular, putting to use the solid experience acquired through his humanistic education. These endeavours also equipped him with an outstanding knowledge of Italian as it was spoken in the fourteenth century, its Golden Age. But by then Pietro had set his sights much higher. While editing Petrarch's *Cose volgari* for Aldo Manuzio, in 1501, and Dante's *Terze rime* — or *Divina Commedia* — in 1502, Pietro knew that the real purpose of these editions was not only to produce reliable versions of the works of the two greatest Italian poets, but also, and more importantly, to establish an audience that would respond favourably to the book he was busy writing: *Gli Asolani*. His new work combined the theme of love with reflections on philosophy. It employed a highly controlled form of Italian, with clear rules modelled on fourteenth-century Tuscan, which was very different from fifteenth-century Italian — typically a mixture of regional idioms and Latin — and its potential readers needed an opportunity to familiarise themselves first with the Italian used by Dante and Petrarch. But the fifteenth-century editions of those two exquisite authors were filled with various accretions, which had to be painstakingly removed to restore the text to its original purity and nobility. This process served a dual purpose: on the one hand, it fostered the development of a language that was on a par with Latin and could be used to create literature in the vernacular to rival the classics; on the other, it prepared a large audience of readers who would receive this literature without any preconceived notion as to its inferiority.

Many years later, in his masterpiece *Prose della volgar lingua*, Pietro still described Latin as the 'most noble language', but made it clear that there was no going back. Anyone who wished to write must now do so in the native tongue. Bembo chose his friend il Magnifico Giuliano, whom we previously met as a young man reflecting on the consequences of his nocturnal misadventures, to serve as his mouthpiece. Giuliano presents the central argument of the *Prose*:

> One may therefore assert, dear Messer Ercole, that when writing one should not use the languages considered most dignified and honourable but rather one's own tongue, provided it is of good quality and worthy of greatness. [...] For if we were to take our memories and transpose them into another language, we should be considered cruel and merciless, like a man who neglects his own mother to support a flighty woman in a faraway place. Since this language of ours is not yet rich and has few authors, whoever writes in the vernacular may claim a large portion of the gratitude afforded to those who first discover all that which is beautiful and admirable.

The metaphor in the above passage is of particular interest, in that it echoes one voiced by Bembo's father in *De Ætna*. Bernardo argued that refusing to serve the Republic was an act of cowardice comparable to abandoning an aged parent. Here, the same image states that betraying one's mother tongue is as reprehensible as lacking gratitude towards one's mother. For Pietro, shaping a language on which to build a new culture demanded a total commitment; it could even be seen as a contribution to society that might take the place of public service.

The underlying idea of the *Prose* took shape during Bembo's Ferraran period, in parallel with the writing of *Gli Asolani*. Pietro alluded to it in a letter to Maria

reader, it bears the signature of Aldo Manuzio but was in fact written by Pietro [Figures 9–10].

As one can easily imagine, such a revolutionary undertaking, which, moreover, rested on the authority of Petrarch's original manuscript, was bound to provoke controversy, suspicion and jealousy. All the more so that Aldo and Pietro again made use of the diacritical marks first introduced by *De Ætna* and, for the first time in the history of printing, the apostrophe. Thus, not only was the text revolutionary, but its graphical innovations made it an easy target for critics, who cast doubt on its faithfulness to the original. Pietro refuted the allegations of his potential critics and justified his linguistic choices with the same virtuosity and systematic approach he would later show in the *Prose*. His *Avviso a gli lettori* strikes a peremptory tone:

> If there is anything herein which our readers do not understand, or regarding which they wish to express some complaint, let them consult Petrarch himself. The great poet transcribed his words with great care onto good paper in a book intended for future generations. I had the opportunity to peruse this work in the house of Pietro Bembo, who also owns other books in the hand of our poet. Rest assured, dear readers, that the present work transcribes his every word letter by letter and without a single error.

The warning at the end of the *Avviso* offers further evidence of the attention that both men devoted to commercial strategies:

> Fare you well and before long expect to discover a Dante no less accurate than this Petrarch, which you will find very valuable. For there were many more inaccurate passages in Dante than in Petrarch, but this book will contain none of the errors one sometimes finds in Petrarch. They have been corrected here and are never found in our publications.

Truth be told, this undertaking, which seems essential to us, was viewed as sacrilegious by many readers with conservative habits and old-fashioned tastes. Without annotations, the text looked raw and naked; the countless punctuation marks were disorienting for the untrained eye; and the poems, rather than appearing in chronological order of writing, as was usual, had been completely reorganised to conform to Petrarch's intentions. In short, Pietro and Aldo had been incredibly daring. The elderly Antonio da Canal, almost eighty at that time, felt himself compelled to pen a moral and philosophical — as well as philological — commentary of Petrarch's *oeuvre*, denouncing the ruses of those he referred to with thinly veiled contempt as 'certain businessmen' (although he did not name them) and accusing them of dragging Petrarch in the mud so as to 'sell more printed paper'.

Those editorial and philological activities were but a first — but nonetheless essential — step in a carefully considered, forward-looking cultural programme, the outline of which was just starting to materialise. A new project was taking shape through philology. It was not the exclusive property of Pietro — it was rooted in broad sections of Venetian culture — but his collaboration with Aldo Manuzio was one of its cornerstones. This project was founded on the constitution of an encyclopaedic sum of knowledge, which was to be both modern and philologically sound, centred on the idea of a language — either Latin or the vernacular — that was

Savorgnan and later referred to it openly in his edition of the two classics of Italian poetry. In July 1502, while staying with Ercole Strozzi at his villa near Ferrara, Pietro transcribed the works of Dante and Petrarch. In August 1502, the Dante was published under the unusual title *Le terze rime di Dante*, but it was the edition of Petrarch published earlier the same year that marked a real turning point for Italian culture. Until then, Aldo Manuzio had published only books in Latin and Greek, with two significant exceptions: the *Epistole* of Saint Catherine of Siena, in 1500, and the previously mentioned *Hypnerotomachia Poliphili*, in 1499. The former was an edition of an important religious work, published in a jubilee year, in the context of a movement to rediscover the great medieval religious texts. It was a shrewd choice, coming as it did only a few years after Girolamo Savonarola's experiment, as the first fluttering of the Reformation was agitating more sensitive souls, but it was devoid of linguistic preoccupations. The second book was truly unique: written in a vernacular Italian modelled on the syntax and morphology of Latin and peppered with neologisms and Hellenisms, it bore little relationship to any existing vernacular, and was in fact a linguistic monster with few descendants, most of them parodies. The Dante and Petrarch were printed immediately after an edition of Virgil and another of Horace.

The new Petrarch had a special connection with the Virgil, which had been issued in April 1501. It was the first book printed by Aldo Manuzio in a small, handy octavo format and using a cursive typeface based on that used by the Roman Curia and the calligraphy of Bartolomeo Sanvito, as mentioned previously. These italic characters were elegant and easy to read, while the book's small size made it handy to carry. Wide, empty margins without glosses or notes allowed readers to add their own comments. The format was inspired by manuscripts of Virgil from the Bembo family library, as indicated by Aldo Manuzio in his introduction to the second edition of the Virgil in 1514: he describes how he discovered several small *enchiridii*, literally, 'books for the hand,' in Bernardo's library.

Those innovations, which can be described as technological, resulted in the arrival on the market of an extraordinary new product, designed to improve its readability and facilitate its circulation. Fifteen copies of the Petrarch were printed on parchment and the rest on paper. The text featured several other crucial improvements. Bembo had obtained two different manuscripts of *Rerum vulgarium fragmenta*, which he compared to establish the ideal version. He recorded the result of this research in a manuscript now in the Vatican Library (Vat Lat. 3197, in Bembo's hand). He had almost completed the task (reaching poem 337), when, by a stroke of luck, he received a third manuscript from the Santasofia family of Padua (it is now in the Vatican Library ms. Vat Lat. 3195). He quickly realised that it was in Petrarch's own hand. With the help of this valuable new source, he finished his transcription and revised what he had already written. Much later, in 1545, he succeeded in purchasing the manuscript for his collection. This project allowed Bembo to significantly improve his command of fourteenth-century Italian, which was thereby re-emerging in a very pure form after an interval of almost two centuries. An indication of this new awareness is apparent in an *Avviso* that was appended to the work as a separate document. Addressed to the

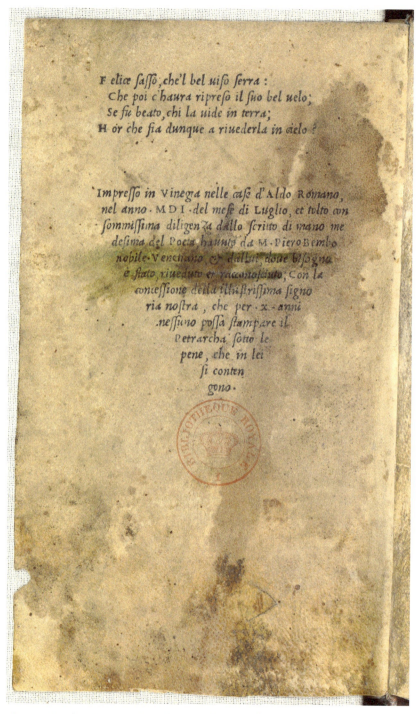

Fig. 9. Pietro Bembo, *Le cose volgari di messer Francesco Petrarcha*, Impresso in Vinegia nelle case d'Aldo Romano, nel anno M D I del mese di Luglio, c. Ai r, Bibliothèque nationale de France, Paris.

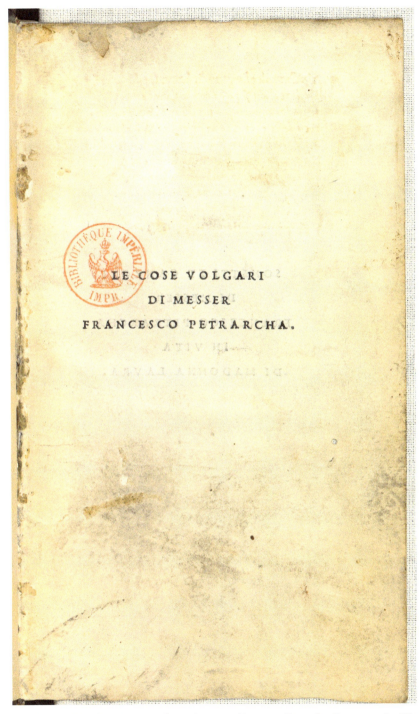

Fig. 10. Pietro Bembo, *Le cose volgari di messer Francesco Petrarcha*, Impresso in Vinegia nelle case d'Aldo Romano, nel anno M D I del mese di Luglio, c. Ziii r, Bibliothèque nationale de France, Paris.

simultaneously dignified, clear and precise. In that time of serious political — and later religious — divisions, society needed sophisticated linguistic tools to facilitate the circulation of ideas and the exchange of opinions, and to overcome mutual misunderstandings. This was a grand Humanist undertaking in the broadest sense, far more ambitious in scope than the civic Humanism of Bernardo's generation, whose chief purpose was to glorify and serve Venice. Recalling the teachings of men slightly older than himself, such as Ermolao Barbaro, Bembo helped realise the dream of a European republic of letters. In his view, all these elements were connected: precise language, achieved by means of exacting philological research, was a necessary precondition to conceptual precision. It enabled the development of a philosophy based on a renewed understanding of Aristotle, free from the accretions of medieval and fifteenth-century commentaries, which was radically different from the hazy Neoplatonic doctrine of Lorenzo il Magnifico's time. Formal, sterile elegance as an end in itself was thus rejected in favour of a precise language suitable for use in all areas of human enquiry, but especially the sciences, in which Pietro had a keen interest, as demonstrated by *De Ætna* and confirmed by his large collection of scientific instruments. The variety of his interests was well known, which explains why, in 1543, several years before he died, Francesco Maurolico, an author from Messina, dedicated to him his *Cosmographia*, a book in which he deplored his contemporaries' lack of interest in science and the parlous state of the works of ancient mathematicians and cosmographers.

Ermolao Barbaro and Angelo Poliziano were the tutelary geniuses of that idea of culture, which spread rapidly under the impetus of a group of their Italian and European disciples, connected by a vast epistolary network. However, Pietro and Aldo went a step further than those two great scholars by discarding some of their teachings, in particular their views about language. What was needed was a language that was as universal as possible. That language was Latin, of course, but not the eclectic Latin theorised by Ermolao and Poliziano. The two friends understood that the only version of Latin applicable to the whole continent was a pure and rigorous one derived from a single model, namely the writings of Cicero, though for some that implied a reverence that sometimes bordered on the superstitious. This was the view of Erasmus of Rotterdam, for instance; in 1529, he satirised the excessive obsequiousness of those disciples of Cicero's eloquence in a book entitled *Ciceronianus*. However, as early as 1512, Bembo set out his views on the authors he considered worthy of being imitated in the pamphlet *De imitatione*, which took the form of a debate between himself and Giovan Francesco Pico della Mirandola. He contrasted the latter's eclectic theories with his own preference for Virgil and Cicero. Clearly, the argument was not just one of taste, but reflected a political and social vision of the new European civilisation emerging in the wake of the collapse of Italian independence, shortly before the outbreak of the Protestant Reformation, the portents of which had been obvious for some time. It was thus no surprise when, in 1513, Leo X named Pietro to the prestigious position of secretary in charge of composing papal *brevi*, which were short letters, or 'briefs', regarding everyday matters. Though less formal than a *bulla pontificalis*, a brief was nevertheless written in Latin. Henceforth, they would be written in the style of Cicero, that is, in a pure Latin free of regional or local influences, which could be imposed throughout Europe without giving rise to resentments, mutual incomprehension, divergent interpretations or misunderstandings. This has been aptly described as the emergence of a Rome–Venice axis based principally on style and language. Of course, the role of Venice as the European capital of printing and the existence within its territory of an institution as prestigious as the University of Padua facilitated such a dialogue, thanks to the presence of scholars from all over Europe, as well as the dissemination of their ideas and writings. The shape taken by this new codification of language and far-reaching philology has been described as the 'mirage [...] of a Catholic, and therefore universal, civic perspective'.

During his Ferrara period, Bembo wrote a philological treatise, which was published only many years later. On 14 February 1504, Pietro obtained permission for a book entitled *De corruptis poetarum locis*. This title was quintessentially humanistic, as was the idea of devoting an entire book to the correction of corrupted or altered passages of classical poetry. The aim of this type of books was to propose solutions for incorrect or problematic passages, either by comparing different versions of the same text or through conjecture. However, Pietro's contribution to the genre remained in manuscript form for over a quarter of a century; it was finally printed in 1530, with the title *De Virgilii Culice et Terentii fabulis*. Its scope was limited to the *Culex*, attributed to Virgil, and Terence, who had provided the initial inspiration for Bembo's intellectual journey. Pietro dedicated it to Ercole Strozzi, a friend from Ferrara, who was long dead at the time of publication but still alive in 1503, when the book was initially conceived and written. For Pietro, that year was still full of the memory of a trip he made to Rome in May 1502 with two friends, Valerio Superchio, a medical doctor and astrologer, and Vincenzo Querini, during which the latter, following the practice of that time, received his doctorate from the hands of the pope after a public presentation and discussion of his philosophical conclusions.

On returning to Ferrara in October, Bembo moved into Ercole Strozzi's villa on the outskirts of the city, and stayed for more than a year. The *De Virgilii Culice* transports the reader amidst the overgrown ruins of Rome. It employs the literary device of a fictional discussion between Ermolao Barbaro and Pomponio Leto, which notionally took place in 1492. The task of linking the various generations and temporal planes falls to the narrator, Tommaso Fedra Inghirami. Tommaso, born in Volterra in 1470, was Pietro's contemporary and a student of Pomponio Leto. He moved to Rome and, in 1510, became the prefect of the Vatican Library, while pursuing a career as a scholar and Humanist. He earned the nickname 'Fedra' after playing the role of Phaedra in the eponymous play by Seneca. Raphael painted a famous portrait of him [Figure 11]. Pomponio Leto was a Humanist and antiquarian who founded an academy, the acclaimed Academia Pomponiana (also known as the Academia Romana). The school ran into numerous problems, and was finally shut down in 1468 on the pretext that its disciples were conspiring to assassinate the Venetian Pope Paul II. The members of the Academia dispersed; many of them, including Pomponio, found refuge in Venice under the protection of the Corner family, especially Giorgio Corner, brother of Caterina Queen of Cyprus and *domina*

Fig. 11. Raphael, *Portrait of Fedra Inghirami*, 1514–16, oil on wood, 89.5 × 62.8 cm, Galleria Palatina, Florence. Photo Scala, Florence — courtesy of the Ministero the Ministero Beni e Att. Culturali

Aceli ('Lady of Asolo'), the court at which *Gli Asolani* are set. In essence, to write about the Rome–Venice axis Bembo needed to situate it near the beginning of the century or earlier, in the 1460s or 1470s.

As they strolled among the ruins of imperial Rome, the Venetian Bembo and the Roman (by adoption) Pomponio discovered a desolate landscape filled with devastated buildings and mangled, mutilated statues. That vision inspired a melancholy reflection on the timeless theme of *ubi sunt*. Where were they now, those once-powerful, famous and respected men and women to whom these broken and dismembered statues were dedicated? Similarly, of the countless temples and theatres of ancient Rome, all that remained were empty corpses. Pietro had no way of knowing that this simile — the city as corpse — would be dramatically illustrated a quarter of a century later. On 11 August 1527, several months after the sack of Rome, he wrote to his friend Antonio Tebaldeo, who was in straitened circumstances and had asked him for money: 'I urge you to forsake the poor corpse of beautiful Rome and come to the land where I live.' Rome, the splendid capital of the first two decades of the sixteenth century, was as dead as imperial Rome. This time, however, it was not only the statues and buildings that had fallen, but also a whole world of shared relationships and aspirations, the dream of a universal and triumphant Church and a common Humanist republic. All that remained were smoking ruins, echoing with the cries of women and children raped and slaughtered by the furious Germans, and the agonising certainty that nowhere was safe, since the central symbol of Christianity had been laid to waste; everything was perishable, uncertain, transient and unsettled.

In 1527, Rome was a sad but distant memory for Pietro. At the time of *De Virgilii Culice*, however, the grand programme of rediscovery of the artistic and literary heritage of Antiquity was still very much alive. So many of the classical poets' writings, like ancient statues, lay *mutilati decurtatique*, disfigured and debased after centuries of being ignored and forgotten. Classical Rome needed to be brought back to life. That was the programme laid out in 1519 by Pietro, Raphael and Baldassarre Castiglione in a *Lettera* to Pope Leo X. At the time, Raphael was caught up in an ambitious project to illustrate and reproduce all the monuments of ancient Rome. The pope had outlawed excavations of any kind in Rome, but the painter of Urbino busied himself nonetheless with pencil and paper, recording the city's antiquities so as to be able to study them and use them as models for a scheme of urban and architectural renewal. Rome, in his view, was only then recovering from the barbarianism into which it had descended following the Gothic invasion. What remained at present of the splendour of imperial Rome? Nothing, Raphael and Castiglione contended, in perfect agreement with Bembo (the opinion was in fact quite common among men of culture at that time): 'this noble fatherland is almost a corpse [... and] terribly mangled'. For long, it had been thought that Rome was eternal and that she would escape the greedy hands of fate. But this was an illusion: fate had sunk its teeth into her and gnawed and teared at her prosperous body until all that was left were 'bare bones without flesh'. Her marbles were crushed to make lime for graceless buildings devoid of any guiding principle and doomed to crumble rapidly. *Pulvis et umbra*, wrote Horace: we are dust and shadows. In this case, the powder was crushed marble and the shadows were the great minds of Antiquity, for 'all of Rome [...] is built with the lime extracted from ancient marbles.' But Bembo, Raphael and Castiglione knew perfectly well that the real issue was peace: a long-awaited and much-desired peace, whose seeds their *Lettera* invited Leo X to sow. The decline of the arts — and with them, measure and grace — had begun during the wars of the late imperial age. In recent years, the Italian people had been decimated by new wars. The holy pontiff had a duty to bring peace, but peace without beauty, harmony, order and poetry would be worthless.

As we have seen, it was hoped that the revival of classical culture would help resolve differences and encourage universal dialogue. Pietro's linguistic and philological activism thus coincided with the architectural activism of Raphael and many other artists working in Rome. The fundamental question, however, involved more than architecture and literature, for it touched upon the principle of a world in the measure of man or, rather, the idea of man as the measure of all things. Bembo, Castiglione and Raphael invoked the metaphor of the city as a corpse (which, though dead, is still a body), an image that was common in the writings of the humanists, who were fond of noting similarities between different natural orders. In several of Leonardo's drawings of floods, for instance, gushing waterfalls and violent gusts of wind are depicted as a woman's wild hair. Both Leonardo and Leon Battista Alberti imagined a system of urban water distribution based the circulatory system in the human body. The microcosm of the human body thus mirrored the macrocosm of the city and vice-versa, in an ideal of harmony that verged on the utopian. Chapter XI of the *Lettera* explains the book's ultimate aim, the restoration of classical order and harmony, the same ideal that underpins Pietro's philological activities. In the following passage, Castiglione and Raffaello summarily dismiss the Gothic style, with its proliferation of gargoyles and crickets and its plethora of strange, monstrous creatures that populated what a famous medievalist has termed the 'fantastical Middle Ages':

> The Germans, it seems, started to revive that art [i.e. architecture], but their ornaments were ugly and unequal to the beautiful style of the Romans, who not only built beautiful structures, but also adorned them with beautiful cornices, frescoes, architraves and columns with ornately sculpted capitals and bases, whose dimensions corresponded to the proportions of man and woman. The Germans' only ornaments [...] were often clumsy figures with folded legs, which served to hold up roof beams, or strange animals and unattractive foliage with a nonsensical appearance.

The Gothic period erred in that it ceased to view man — and woman — as the basic unit of measure determining the perfect proportions of the world. It was time to revive that idea. Moreover, a technology was available — inasmuch as architecture is a technological process based on a project, that is, a mathematical and proportional projection — which could be used to shape the world of man, without allowing the latter to dominate the former. Could there be a better definition of the programme of Humanism?

But fate had something else in mind. On Good Friday, 6 April 1520, 'jealous' death 'carried off the young master', Raphael, who had won the admiration of scholars, and more particularly artists and architects, for presenting 'the ancient buildings of Rome in a book, just as Ptolemy described the world, depicting their proportions, their shapes and their ornaments so clearly that to look at them was to see ancient Rome,' in the words of Marcantonio Michiel — an art collector to whom we owe a valuable inventory of Bembo's collection — from both his journal and a letter of 11 April 1520 to Antonio Marsilio. In the letter, he noted in passing that 'the death of Mr Agustino Gisi [Chigi], who expired last night, was much less of a loss to the world.' In other words both the prince of painters and his patron, the richest banker in the world, died in the space of a few days. Leo X died the following year. The most beautiful, lively and intense season of the Renaissance was drawing to a close. When he brought out a second edition of the *Lettera* in 1530, after Rome was sacked and laid to ruin by mercenaries, Pietro may have been hoping to breathe new life into that project and revive the goal of developing a universal language capable of superseding the vicious divides that had opened up in the intervening years. The banner of Humanism, though bloodied and torn, was again raised.

CHAPTER 4

Three Women Seated around the Heart

Venice looked kindly on both lovers and assassins. Love and death, those two faithful companions, met often in its labyrinth of alleys, malodorous *sottoporteghi* (porticos) and dark *campielli* (little piazzas) overhung by decrepit, crooked houses of crumbling brick, their windows poorly shielded by rotten shutters that barely concealed the human suffering within. These houses were closely crowded and interlocked like the pieces of a puzzle or the diseased cells of a tumour. They were inhabited by gondoliers and porters with limbs deformed by their daily toil, prostitutes infected with the French disease (syphilis), soldiers maimed in one of the Serenissima's many wars, typographers and printers with eyes grown dim from long days of staring at the press. No one paid the slightest attention to the sight of a puddle of blood slowly trickling down a lane, while hurried, fugitive footsteps receded into the distance. Nor did they notice the muffled splash of some heavy object falling into a canal, announcing that yet another poor soul has been consigned for all eternity to the lagoon's brackish embrace, and would never again need to worry about his next meal. A woman, swathed in a fine black veil, furtively meeting a young nobleman was even less noteworthy. It was important to be careful nonetheless. Venice was full of spies, and sooner or later every secret became public knowledge. Rumours were the currency of conversation in barbershops and spice merchants' stalls. If even the government's best kept secrets were not safe from gossip, an illicit love affair was still less so.

Nowadays, Campo San Trovaso is a romantic spot. To one side lies a picturesque brick and wood *squero*, or traditional boatyard, with a wooden loggia overflowing with red geraniums. The canal gently laps the edge of the yard. Behind it, an expanse of grass separates the shore from the church of San Trovaso. Low houses surround the field, in the middle of which is a wellhead of white marble. In Pietro's time, the area was certainly less attractive, due to the noise of the workshops and the Giudecca nearby, but that made it all the more suitable for whispered confessions, surreptitious glances and furtive caresses. It was here that a young poet and a married noblewoman, Pietro Bembo and Maria Savorgnan, secretly met and exchanged letters, short messages or sonnets. If unable to come in person, they sent a trusted servant. The year was 1500 to 1501. Bembo had recently ended a long love affair, which had left deep scars, as only a first love can.

She was jealous. Very jealous. Jealous of his memories and of the nameless woman he seemed unable to forget, despite his protestations to the contrary. Their love was a study in contrasts: rash, risky, passionate and, of course, literary. He was getting ready to define the laws of the Italian language and of poetry; she wrote animated letters in vernacular Venetian, a dialect utterly unlike the highly controlled Italian favoured by Pietro. She was also the author of some interesting verses. And she did not hesitate to reprimand her brilliant lover, correcting and scolding him in turn. She didn't like some of his verses: he must revise, correct and amend them.

But their love was first and foremost a tale of passions, subterfuges, quarrels, disappointments and intense surges of desire. She had a keen sense of *mise en scène* and directed her lover with consummate skill:

> Tonight you must do what I wrote in my letter two days ago. Come at one-thirty to Campo San Trovaso and look for a light in the highest windows. Come as usual under the protection of your escort [...]. If I cannot speak to you tonight, I shall tell you tomorrow at what time the window will be closed and you can come.

She imagined various expedients to circumvent her jealous guardian with the help of servants and friends, despite the fact that they sometimes took advantage of the errand to pursue their own flirtations, as the unreliable Cola Bruno was wont to do: 'Send C. to Campo San Trovaso every night after ten, and I shall do the same with F. But not today.'

San Trovaso was also where their love ended. Maria concluded her seventy-seventh and last letter to her lover with an anguished sonnet, *Hor ch'è estinta la fiama e sciolto il nome*, next to which Bembo wrote, 'verses from San Trovaso'. But what paroxysms their passion reached before that time! He sent her gloves from Spain and bouquets of roses; she replied with 'a bunch of basil and a certain herb' wrapped in a handkerchief, warning him that the 'string is made of hair, since I was drying my hair while writing to you and felt a sudden urge to do this'. She invented signs to deliver to him: a black silk thread indicated a particular time when they could meet. Friends and relations joined into the lovers' game: a certain Menega was in charge of making sure that 'you enter by the window; as long as I am out, she will keep you in a place in the house where you will not be seen. After I go to bed, you can leave the room and join me.' Sometimes things did not go so smoothly. She had a jealous husband, or, as a researcher has suggested recently, perhaps a guardian (Maria may have been the widow of Giacomo Savorgnan). And even a stupid man can be dangerous at times.

One night, a stranger came to the Savorgnan house, and the diligent guardian of Maria's virtue became convinced that she was in love with him. Bernardino, for that was the guardian's name, was not just stupid in appearance: he never suspected Bembo. Maria, with great aplomb, organised to meet her lover at the Rialto, with the pretext of exchanging books or attending readings at innocent soirées. But Bernardino, plagued by suspicion, sensed that she was hiding something. He could be frightening, if necessary. The tired old ox then turned into a raging lion:

> After that person had departed, he became like an unchained lion, searching

> everywhere in the house. I was in the room above the canal and aware of nothing until he entered all of a sudden. Because of Donata's stupidity, he lifted the bench where the trundle bed is kept and found the ladder. Imagine how I felt: I had lost all credibility and didn't know what to do. Our guide, who keeps the key to a certain room with a barred window, which is above the bedchambers, said that B. took it with many threats, and warned him never to speak to anyone of it.

She concluded this lively, entertaining account with words full of childish naiveté: 'Render a thousand graces to this letter and kiss it, for it is pretty'.

Throughout their turbulent affair — which seems almost to foreshadow the comedy *La Venexiana*, with its sequences of signals, open and shut windows, wily servants and ladders for climbing into bedrooms — Maria, like an experienced stage director, told Pietro exactly where to go, what to wear, how long to wait in a certain tower, and so on:

> I may be able to come out and speak with you today, but if not today then certainly tomorrow, at Chami's or the two towers. You must go first so that no one recognises you; you will be led to a sort of tower in which you must stay until I arrive. If all goes according to plan, you can immediately send away the boat that brought you there, as I can take you wherever you want to go in mine.

She had to explain everything very clearly, since Pietro's inexperience and lack of prudence risked giving them away. 'You almost let someone see you; was it really so hard to make sure no one recognised you? I am so worried that I don't know what to say,' she scolded. Caught out like a schoolboy, Pietro defended himself: 'It's all your fault: you were the one who insisted I wear the neighbour's clothes. If I obey you and it doesn't go well, I am not the one to blame!' Once, she had a fever and could not see him. He, on the other hand, spent the time agreeably, singing and having fun, which naturally made her very angry. She could not forgive him: 'I am ill and you sing songs. So be it... I console myself with the thought that you will have to repent your sins.' She added, 'You amuse and enjoy yourself; you give no thought to me since every evening there are people singing under your windows. I would be far more surprised to hear that you ever rise before five, given the life that you live'. He drew on his well-stocked rhetorical arsenal for his response:

> It is now four o'clock and Taddeo Toscano has just left my house. He stood underneath my window and regaled me with his harmonious song. I invited him up, and he sang many beautiful tunes to give my heart pleasure. But no song can relieve its longing and restore its happiness but that which comes from the one who is the source of all my pleasure, as a tree grows from its roots.

On another occasion, and for the same reason, Pietro mischievously replied: 'I was happy to hear you sing, though you were not forced to. It is a thing that people do not usually do when they are as ill as you claim to be.' However, his main crime, in Maria's eyes, was that he had not forgotten his first love: 'You cannot say that by adding another nail to your heart you have removed the first'. That accusation prompted a curt response from Pietro:

> I was very melancholy today, and became even more so when Cola arrived with your letters, or rather your wounds, which made me doubt my salvation

for a long while. If you act in this way to revenge yourself for an offence I have caused you, or to teach me to fear what I do not fear much, as I have never knowingly offended you, and have always taken care to do nothing that might bring you displeasure, then, if that is the case, revenge yourself with words and not actions, and be harsher on paper than in your heart. [...] However, if these scenes become a habit, you may soon find that you do not only what you wish but far more. Indeed, like those children who hold a little bird tightly in the hand, believing that they are pleasing themselves, yet soon realise that they have killed it, you believe that you are tormenting me when in fact you are killing me, for I feel that this anguish may become too much for me to bear.

Jealousy was a constant in their relationship; in his final letter to Maria, Bembo explained in no uncertain terms that by ridiculing his first love she had proved herself to be exactly like his former mistress. The letter ends on a melodramatic note:

It pains me to discover in you a soul less elevated than I once thought, since you dissemble openly and without cause against such a pure soul. For years I have been searching for what twice I thought I had found: a sure and faithful heart. But I shall search no longer, for I now believe that all women are cut from the same cloth. My sacred faithfulness, founded in the ardent desire that you know so well, was not like other men's, whereas yours towards me is exactly like that of the other woman whom you are so fond of mocking.

He was becoming the real Pietro Bembo. His love for Maria mingled with the writing of *Gli Asolani*; part of that treatise is present in the above tableau, which constantly alternated the two faces of love, the bitter and the ecstatic.

It was also a period of intense collaboration with Aldo Manuzio, whose workshop was just then preparing the new editions of Petrarch and Dante.

This sacred lead of ours, as you call it, to which one must pay particular attention in these times and in this city, has prompted me to modify my behaviour. Suffice it to say that it has curbed my zeal in satisfying my modest and honest desires.

The lead of the type, and the huge amount of work involved in printing books at a time when the trade was fast expanding, drove a wedge between the lovers. When not preoccupied with the lead, Pietro was busy writing: 'I imagine you must be working on your *Asolani*, and that is why you didn't wait for me.' For Pietro, however, *Gli Asolani* was the yardstick by which he measured the intensity of their love, as if he could experience life only when filtered through literature:

How sweet and dear it would be if all your thoughts were open to me as mine are to you, so that I might see in your heart, and you in mine, as easily I see my own heart and you yours! Only then will our love have reached its zenith. And if, as a woman who desires every perfection, it distresses you to hear me say that our love has not yet reached the point it should, look at what is said on this topic by the two perfect lovers discussing their happiness in Book II of *Gli Asolani*.

This variation on one of Pietro's favourite themes, the perfect correspondence of feelings, appears repeatedly in his letters to Maria:

The gods know in what spirit I speak to you; how I wish they would let you look inside my heart. You would be able see it as clearly as if it were made of crystal, and you would be happy for having seen it.

Literature was a third protagonist in their relationship. Maria sent her verses to Pietro, and he sent his to her, asking her to amend and polish them. At first she was taken aback: 'How could any file of mine be suitable for cleansing and polishing your verse?' 'I love your sonnets, I love them very much. Whether they are of value is for you to determine.' With time, however, she became more confident and assertive; if she was not convinced, she said so: 'The song is beautiful, but you should revise it; you can certainly improve it.' She even became angry and combative when her proud, stubborn friend refused to listen to her: 'You don't want to change this verse and you say it is different, because Petrarch says *Con questo pensier* and you say *Col primo*. I am embarrassed for you, Pietro Bembo. Do as you wish, then, but I don't like it.'

He sent her 'tre sorele', probably the three songs of Lavinello from the *Asolani*, which she corrected, suggesting some original changes to the text. In his response, he chided her for not spending more time on her own poems, which also needed polishing: 'I wish you would devote more effort to your own writings, and improve them where they are imperfect, like the verses I sent you this morning, which in places do not satisfy me.' It was for Maria that Pietro started to take notes on the vernacular which would later form the kernel of the *Prose della volgar lingua*: 'I have written some notes on language, as I told you I planned following your request with regard to your letters.'

Meanwhile, their love was slowly perishing. Maria left for Ferrara in February 1501 and Pietro stayed in Venice. They reproached each other more and more bitterly, and the tone of their letters went from fresh and lively to solemn and grave. Each felt the other did not love enough, and read doubt, pretexts and complications into the other's actions.

In the words of Carlo Dionisotti, it was 'not [...] a spring-like explosion of life so much as [...] a midday affirmation of an awareness of sunset.' Pietro had matured and was ready to take on a public role as guide to the world of literature. Maria, although probably just as mature, was confined to her role as a woman and wife. They were both searching for a way to escape through the heart and the mind, Dionisotti notes. Petrarch allowed them to kindle a love, which, although in many ways it resembled a romance, rose above the comic aspects of love and a certain denial of woman in Humanism. It was simultaneously a sublimated experience and a real one, based on a correspondence of refined passions and a recognition of the nobility of woman. It was also an affair situated at the juncture between youth and maturity, and blessed with a miraculously harmonious combination of liveliness, spontaneity, joy and sadness, as well as literary and intellectual dimensions. The foundation and inspiration for Pietro and Maria's relationship was provided by an easy-going Petrarchism, which provided the words their love needed to express itself without silencing the voice of the heart, and allowed it to flow as free and fresh as water from a spring, especially in her letters. Conversely, Pietro had a tendency to trouble that clear stream by adopting a professorial tone, though he never managed to completely dissimulate the explosion of life that marked the months during which Cupid steered the two Venetians 'wherever he wanted'. Pietro declared that he would never love another woman, but, like many who have uttered such words, he was wrong. A new passion awaited him amidst the mists and swamps of Ferrara, where his last love had died a slow death.

On the second of February 1502, an elegantly dressed couple entered Ferrara on horseback. It was just before Lent, and the couple made the most of the opportunity to show off their most sumptuous clothes before the period of penitence began. The man rode a bay horse caparisoned with crimson and gold velvet. He was dressed all in velvet, with black velvet shoes and a hat with gold lettering — possibly a motto, like the one in the *Portrait of a Nobleman* by Bartolomeo Veneto [Figure 12].

Astride her white horse bedecked in crimson cloth trimmed with pearls and gold and silver thread, the woman was even more elegant and graceful. She wore

> a *camora* [long jacket] of crimson satin trimmed with brocade ribbon and a *sbernia* [cape] of a rich and curly gold brocade lined with ermine. Her coif was finely worked with gold, precious stones and large pearls, and she wore a necklace of diamonds, rubies and large pearls, a large ruby brooch and a very valuable and beautiful pearl pendant.

Expert eyes had estimated the value of her headdress, which was encrusted with diamonds, sapphires and various other gemstones, at thousands of ducats. Departing from Rome, the lady had reached Torre della Fossa the day before, where she was welcomed by the sound of trumpets, fifes and drums.

No wonder, for the lady was none other than Lucrezia Borgia, daughter of Pope Alexander VI and wife of Alfonso d'Este, future Duke of Ferrara. The reigning Duke Ercole, surrounded by a large retinue of dignitaries, welcomed her in person and accompanied her to Ferrara on the ducal barge. The city was in a fever pitch of excitement. Alfonso, escorted by a delegation of ambassadors and courtiers, had left in early December to fetch her from the papal city. The couple's arrival had been awaited for months: the excitement was palpable and the people were impatient to set eyes on that beautiful young woman, the enigmatic offspring of a scandalous family. Lucrezia's retinue was impressive: crossbowmen in red and white livery, with feathered caps in the French style, *legisti* (lawyers), representatives of the various trades, twenty carts filled with noble ladies and drawn by white horses, and seventy mules carrying her wedding trousseau.

Among the ladies in her retinue was Elisabetta Gonzaga, Duchess of Urbino. The Marchesa of Mantua, Isabella d'Este awaited her at the Palazzo Ducale. At regular intervals along the way, the triumphant cortège stopped at four stations where allegorical representations were given under canopied arches: they figured three goddesses holding golden apples, an allegory of the Hesperides; Hercules and Cupid; Mercury with the nymphs; and a bullock ridden by a nymph and surrounded by nymphs, satyrs and bullocks, a clear reference to the powerful red bull in the arms of the Borgia family. At each station, poets recited verses in praise of the new couple. On 3 February, a great ball was held in honour of the bride; she presided over the festivities seated on a throne draped in gold cloth and flanked by the Marchesa of Mantua and the Duchess of Urbino. When the dancing stopped,

Fig. 12. Bartolomeo Veneto, *Portrait of a Gentleman*, c. 1512, oil on wood, 73.5 × 53 cm, Galleria Nazionale d'Arte antica, Rome. Photo Scala, Florence; courtesy of the Ministero Beni e Att. Culturali

the noble ladies and gentlemen continued to the Palazzo del Podestà della Ragione [...] which was decked out for the occasion with tribunes, houses and castles of painted wood, and there, in addition to countless entertainments, songs, games and Moorish dances, there was given a performance of a comedy by Plautus, entitled *Epidicus*.

But that was not the end of it: on Friday the fourth, there was another play by the same author, *Bacchides*. On Sunday the sixth, after Mass, during which a bishop dispatched by the bride's father presented Alfonso with a gold sword and cap trimmed with ermine and pearls, thereby conferring the duchy upon him, the guests attended a performance of *Miles gloriosus*. The next day, the enjoyed another play by Plautus, *Asinaria*, followed by *Casina* on the eighth day.

Lucrezia's marriage magnificently illustrated Renaissance civilisation at its apogee. It featured all the characteristic elements of that unique period: luxurious clothing and jewels, wild parties with dancing, music and singing, mythological imagery, love poetry, temporary constructions, a love of the theatre and classical literature, and the dense web of dynastic alliances among great ruling families — Este, Gonzaga, Montefeltro, Borgia and so on. In the background, as if to highlight the magnificence of the display, one imagines the secret manoeuvres of a group of devious, one might even say cynical, characters: the enigmatic Lucrezia, the dreaded Cesare, who had just declared war against the rightful Duke of Urbino, and the long shadow of their fearsome father, Alexander VI. The pope, then in his sixties, was deeply infatuated with the beautiful Giulia Farnese, a girl of fifteen; in exchange for her favours and the scent of her nubile skin, she requested a cardinalship for her brother Alessandro. This was the same Alessandro who later became Pope Paul III and made Pietro Bembo a cardinal. How many destinies crossed paths in the early days of the year 1502!

Lucrezia was beautiful. In the enthusiastic words of the Ferraran chronicler Bernardino Zambotto, 'she was beautiful of mien, with lovely, merry eyes, erect in her demeanour and her role, attentive, very careful, very cultivated, cheerful, pleasant and kind'. Nicolò Cagnola, the secretary of the French ambassador to the court of Este, recorded a more objective view:

> This famous lady, Madama Lucrezia Borgia, is married and is around twenty-five years of age; she is of medium build, somewhat thin in appearance, with a longish face, a beautiful nose and profile, golden hair, light eyes, a rather wide mouth with very white teeth, a frank, white bosom adorned with decency and good taste, and she is of a constantly cheerful and smiling character.

A lock of her blond hair is preserved in a glass case mounted on a candelabra-like foot, made in 1928 by the goldsmith Alfredo Ravasco [Figure 13]. According to legend, the lock was found between the pages of Lucrezia's letters to Pietro Bembo, preserved in manuscript S.P.II.100 in the Biblioteca Ambrosiana; its existence has been known since 1685. The gift of a lock of hair was indeed alluded to in a letter from Pietro to Lucrezia, dated 14 July 1503. It was likely a widespread custom, since Maria also gave Pietro a lock of her hair. As noted above, Pietro returned to Ferrara in October 1502 and stayed at Ercole Strozzi's villa in Ostellato, outside the city. The new duchess rapidly became the recipient of compliments and gifts from the

Fig. 13. Lucrezia Borgia's hair (1480–1519), 1928. Veneranda Pinacoteca Ambrosiana, Milan. © Veneranda Biblioteca Ambrosiana/DeAgostini Picture Library/Scala, Florence

writers at court, including Strozzi, Tebaldeo and Ludovico Ariosto. In August 1506, Ariosto wrote an eclogue (*Dove vai, Melibeo, dove sí ratto*) celebrating Alfonso and Lucrezia under the guise of a pastoral fiction and praising them for their wisdom in transforming the duchy into an oasis of peace. With a bit of sycophantic flattery, Alfonso's ferociousness toward his brothers was reinterpreted as good governance. Indeed, in the time of uncertainty that followed the death of Duke Ercole, a quarrel broke out between Alfonso's brothers Giulio and Ippolito, the result of which was that Giulio was blinded — a crime that was never punished. This was followed by a failed plot, which resulted in the execution by beheading of all the conspirators but Giulio and a third brother, Ferrante. Ferrara's most splendid age thus ended in bloodshed. Shortly thereafter, on 6 June 1508, Pietro's friend Ercole Strozzi was found stabbed to death by the side of the road. What was his crime? Perhaps that he was a spy in the service of the Duke of Mantua; more likely that he had facilitated an illicit relationship between the Duke and Lucrezia. Be that as it may, the story of Licoria and Alfenio in Ariosto's eclogue offered a barely disguised account of Lucrezia's arrival in Ferrara, while listing her incomparable virtues:

> Lizards were already basking in the sun, while on the warm riverbank young shepherds went searching for the first violets, when, with wise reserve, Licoria arrived among that congress of women whose beauty was almost divine. There she married Alfenio, and his father, who was then still alive, gave a celebration more sumptuous than any which had been seen before. I saw the other women, and I saw her, sometimes alone, sometimes together, every time in a different dress. Like tin next to silver, copper next to gold, a field poppy next to a rose, a wan willow next to a green laurel were all the others next to the bride […]. But those who knew her best extolled less her angelic beauty than her genius and her holy works. (vv. 241–67)

Ludovico Ariosto, future author of *Orlando furioso*, offered a variation on a cliché, according to which the blond, smiling Lucrezia's intellectual and moral qualities surpassed her extraordinary beauty.

In fact, the aim was to draw attention away from the delicate question of her paternity as well as her previous marriages: to Giovanni Sforza, ruler of Pesaro, which was annulled in 1497, and to the Duke of Bisceglie, Alfonso d'Aragon, who was assassinated by henchmen sent by Lucrezia's brother, supposedly with her complicity. Not to mention the existence of a son born from an affair with a servant, and rumours of an incestuous relationship with her father and brother. It was even said that on 31 October 1501, after her marriage to Alfonso was celebrated, while the envoys who had come from Ferrara to salute the bride and report back to Ercole were still in Rome, Lucrezia attended an orgy organised by Valentino, though possibly only as a spectator. Fifty courtesans were invited to his apartment in the Vatican while the pope was present. Lighted candelabras were placed on the floor and chestnuts spread on it, which the naked women crawled on all fours to pick up. Prizes were awarded to the guests who demonstrated their virility by copulating with the largest number of women. All this was to be kept under a blanket of silence as thick as the velvets and brocades hanging from the walls of the Palazzo Ducale during the week of wedding festivities.

Fig. 14. Pinturicchio, *St Catherine's Disputation*, 1492–94, Apostolic Palace, Borgia Apartments, Vatican (detail: presumed portrait of Lucrezia Borgia). © 2015 Photo Scala, Florence

Pietro complied with his duties as a courtier and offered poems in praise of the duchess. Had heavy rains caused the River Po to overflow its banks? At once he dashed off the epigram *De Pado exundante*, which explained that the great river had left its bed to admire Lucrezia [Figure 14]. Had she appeared in public wearing a bracelet in the shape of snake? Immediately, Pietro's fertile imagination transformed the bracelet into a real snake, which was turned into a jewel by nymphs on the banks of the River Tage. The Tage, hearing reports of Lucrezia's beauty, sent her the bracelet to adorn herself. This type of flattery is taken to another level entirely in the poem *Ad Lucretiam Borgiam*. Nature, Pietro wrote, decreed that women who receive the largest share of beauty may not also achieve intellectual excellence as well. Conversely, women endowed with a great intellect cannot hope to receive beauty. But Lucrezia flaunted that immutable rule. The poem lists the duchess's many talents: she sang in Italian like a native (the Borgias were in fact Spanish); she composed songs, lyrics and music on her flute; she was so skilful on the lute that her playing could stop the powerful flow of the River Po; she danced so gracefully that even the gods were charmed, and might very well carry her off one day to transform her into a new star in the firmament. Although Bembo frequently mocked lovers who fell prey to the tempests of love while he watched them struggle from the safety of the shore, it was now his turn to succumb and to wander those obscure paths.

FIG. 15. Lorenzo Costa, *Allegory of the Court of Isabella d'Este*, sixteenth century, oil on canvas, 164.5 × 197.5 cm, Musée du Louvre, Paris. Photo © RMN-Grand Palais (Musée du Louvre) / Thierry Le Mage

Pietro was in love with Lucrezia. Even today, the nature of their relationship is not entirely clear. There was certainly a strong literary element: from the moment that Pietro opted for a courtly rather than a political career and chose Petrarch and the theme of love as the distinctive aspects of his activity as a writer at a court where literature reigned supreme, a flirtation of some kind became a physical inevitability, a logical conclusion and a necessary complement. In a word, elected love was part of the role he was fashioning for himself. But one cannot therefore assume that this love was purely literary, though literature certainly played an important part in it. Pietro's first letter to Lucrezia begins with two sonnets and concludes with a reference to the *Asolani*. Five days later, Pietro received a gold coin from Lucrezia, with a request for a motto to be inscribed on it. He suggested the motto 'EST ANIMUM' (devours the soul). After explaining his favourite metaphor of the crystalline heart to Lucrezia, Pietro, possibly inspired by the heat, wrote her a letter on 14 July, which begins with these passionate words:

> I rejoice that each day to increase my fire you cunningly devise some fresh incitement, such as that which encircled your glowing brow today. If you do such things because, feeling some little warmth yourself, you wish to see another burn, I shall not deny that for each spark of yours untold Etnas are raging in my breast.

The hot breath of Etna from Pietro's youth irresistibly rose out of his memories.

A few days later, they were to be apart for a few days; the time had come for Pietro to kiss 'that tender hand which has slain me', and self-pityingly declare 'were I an angel [...] I should be consumed with great pity for any man who loved as much as I. My heart kisses your Ladyship's hand which so soon I shall come to kiss with these lips that are forever forming your name'. These were passionate words indeed. On 19 June, he sent her a sonnet on the theme of the crystal heart and begged her to tell him what she saw when gazing into the crystal of his heart. Her response is guarded but unambiguous:

> Messer Pietro mio, Concerning the desire you have to hear from me regarding the counterpart of your or our crystal as it may rightly be reputed and termed, I cannot think what else to say or imagine save that it has an extreme affinity of which the like perhaps has never been equalled in any age. And may this suffice. And let it be a gospel everlasting.

The meaning is clear, but the words are carefully chosen. Lucrezia's prudence may perhaps prove indirectly that their feelings went beyond platonic friendship or literary flirtation. Pietro's words certainly leave little doubt as to the nature of his love. The fire within him continued to rage: on 5 October, he wrote to Lucrezia that his sole desire was for the fire in which she had placed him to be 'the highest and brightest blaze that in our time ever set a lover's heart alight'. If she ever felt that he did not love her deeply enough, he assured her, she was mistaken. But many obstacles were placed in their way: his travels, her social engagements and, more problematically, the irreducible social distance between them. Consequently, their relationship progressively drifted toward a realm of imagination and memory. Two weeks later, Pietro described this charming nocturnal scene:

> Often I find myself recalling, and with what ease, certain words spoken to me, some on the balcony with the moon as witness, others at that window I shall always look upon so gladly, with all the many endearing and gracious acts I have seen my gentle lady perform.

More upsetting and unpredictable partings lay in store for Pietro, beginning with the death of his brother Carlo. Recalled to Venice on family matters, he took leave of Lucrezia. On 5 January 1504, he wrote from Venice: 'I am sending for my books that I left in Ferrara, and shall not move from here for a while so that at least during these days my elderly and grieving father need not remain bereft of all light, for there is little doubt he needs my comfort. Of my return I shall say no more than that I know not what to say.'

Shortly afterwards, Pietro, when mentioning f.f. — he referred to Lucrezia by these initials, the significance of which has not yet been elucidated, in order to avoid suspicion if his letters were intercepted — wrote that, though unable to see her or speak with her, he still enjoyed 'the thought, the memory of her who encircles my heart each day, each night, every hour, wheresoever I am, whatever my condition.' Their love now existed only in the darkness of night and in the disembodied realm of dream, fantasy and illusion. If they were disappointed and separated in real life, they could always meet elsewhere. Withdrawn from the world in his *villetta* (probably the villa in Noniano), soothed by its protective solitude, he yearned for a world unshackled from the laws of space and time: 'If during this period you chance to find your ears are ringing it will be because I am communing with all those dark things and horrors and tears of yours, or else writing pages about you that will still be read a century after we are gone.' Finally, on 10 February 1505, Pietro took leave of his love in a wonderfully sad and tender letter:

> You must know the first hour I saw you that you penetrated my mind to such a degree that never afterwards have you been able to quit it through any cause. And if I said nothing of this to you for a long time it was because my accursed ill-fortune, never more powerful than when opposing all my deepest desires, decreed it so [...] and although this same ill-fortune is more than ever arrayed against me now, yet have I no fear, for it could never make me so afraid that I could cease to love you and not count you the one dear mistress of my self and my life [...]. And I would ask you to reflect that anyone can love when all fares well and all seems well-disposed, but if instead there are forever a thousand harsh and conflicting things, a thousand separations, a thousand watchmen, a thousand barriers and a thousand walls, then not all can love, and if able to they may not so desire, or if they desire they do not persevere [...]. And when that day comes it will be lovely and precious for us to recall that we were staunch and constant lovers and it will seem to us that we are only truly happy because we share this memory.

Enclosed in the letter was a keepsake for Lucrezia to remember him by, in spite of distance that separated her from him:

> Out of love for me sometimes please deign to wear at night the enclosed Agnus Dei which I once used to wear upon my breast, if you cannot wear it in the day, so that your precious heart's dear abode, which I should gladly stake my

life to kiss but once and long, may at least be touched by this roundel which for so long has touched the abode of mine.

With this gift, which he enjoined her to wear close her heart at night, their love finally reached the land of dreams to which it had been heading for a while.

Was Pietro Bembo capable of true love, one wonders? Perhaps more than his writings indicate. He had many long-lasting and affectionate — but not necessarily romantic — relationships with a number of women, including some of the most fascinating figures of the century, including Isabella d'Este, Veronica Gambara and Vittoria Colonna. But the writings relating to his relationships with Maria Savorgnan, Lucrezia Borgia and Morosina give an impression of aloofness, reserve and slight affectation. For instance, the many verses he composed on the death of Morosina express little grief or intense emotions. After his first love, which seems to have left deep scars, Lucrezia may have been the only woman for whom he temporarily abandoned his carapace of coolly courteous classicism.

Bembo's love affairs with Maria and Lucrezia took place in the early years of the sixteenth century, between 1500 and 1503. Around the same time, Pietro met Isabella d'Este, marchesa of Mantua and wife of Francesco Gonzaga. A highly cultivated woman, Isabella admired the work of Leonardo da Vinci and took a keen interest in the fast-growing publishing industry. In 8 July 1501, she asked her steward in Venice to buy her a copy of the works of Petrarch printed on parchment by Aldo Manuzio. A year later, she wrote to Alberto Pio da Carpi, a friend of Pietro, asking him to persuade the Bembo family to send her the portraits of Dante, Petrarch and Boccaccio in their possession. This marked the beginning of a long and affectionate friendship with Pietro, based on a shared passion for art. The court of Mantua counted many outstanding poets, including Niccolò da Correggio, Paride Ceresara and Tebaldeo. Unlike most noblewomen of her time, Isabella had a study of her own, which she decorated with paintings by Bellini, Mantegna and Lorenzo Costa. Costa painted a famous portrait of her between 1505 and 1506, entitled *Isabella d'Este nel regno di Armonia*, depicting a Garden of Eden where music, art and poetry are cultivated; at the centre, Venus hold up Anteros, god of spiritual, heavenly love, to place a crown of laurels on Isabella's head [Ill. 15].

The duchess loved music and was fond of singing the verses of her favourite poets, accompanied by musicians. On 1 July 1505, Pietro sent her several poems: 'I am sending you ten sonnets and two *strambotti*, which I would be very happy to hear you recite and sing, for I still cherish the memory of your beautiful singing the other night and could imagine no higher honour for my poems.' Bembo tried in vain to obtain one of Giovanni Bellini's works for her. For many years, they corresponded principally about art and literature, in a sort of ideal triangular exchange between Ferrara, Mantua and Urbino, where Isabella's sister-in-law Elisabetta Gonzaga had married the unfortunate Guidubaldo da Montefeltro. From 1512, the letters grew less frequent and less intense, but were still full of affectionate and delightfully witty exchanges. Pietro feigned annoyance with her for asking him to intercede with the pope to allow her to attend Mass at times when it was forbidden, or teasingly complained that she still not sent him a '*bussolino* [...] from her excellent mixture' (probably a perfume or a scented ointment, maybe for the hair). Pietro's sensuality was satisfied by a gift from the marchesa on 23 March 1514: a platter of carp, a prized freshwater fish. The friendly visits, meetings and exchanges of favours continued until Isabella's death, on 30 January 1539.

Her son Cardinal Ercole was also a faithful friend and sponsor of Pietro's: he supported him in his career, which culminated in his election as cardinal despite the opposition of part of the Curia. In particular, his critics objected to his excessive love of women. On 22 January 1539, Nino Sermini, Cardinal Ercole's agent in Rome, wrote to his master about the accusations against Bembo, one of which stood out:

> The only fault they can find is that he lived openly with a woman and had several children with her, and that he lived with another woman after the first one died. And although that is not unusual nowadays, certain evil tongues accuse the cardinal of being a man with a carnal knowledge of the women of this country.

A *Lettera della padrona di Roma a papa Paulo* which was posted in 1544 on Pasquino, an ancient statue standing across from Palazzo Braschi — poems violently criticising the authorities, in this case the Curia, were displayed on the statue, a custom that has survived until today — puts forth the same argument with greater virulence:

> Bembo would turn the world upside down rather than deprive himself of the pleasure of spending his days writing rubbish. He would lay hands on all the medals in Rome to decorate his study in Padua if he could. And he would do anything in his power to enrich his bastard, the son of the woman he claims to love, although the boy is so ugly that he is probably the child of some boatman.

In this passage, a charge of excessive sensuality is combined with attacks on Pietro's writings and on his love of medals and art. The accusation was not entirely unfounded: on 23 August 1542, Pietro wrote to his agent Flaminio Tomarozzo asking him to send him several medals from Rome and enjoining him to maintain the strictest confidentiality regarding this particular sensual indulgence. When running his fingers over the outlines of the bodies, faces and silhouettes on the medals, the cardinal felt the same pleasurable *frisson* as he once did when following a desirable woman through the narrow lanes of Venice, the fog and mist of Ferrara, the steep stairways of Urbino, the palaces of Rome or the tranquil air of Villa Bozza. In truth, art and sensuality were two faces of the same medal for Bembo — the man who loved Raphael and Lucrezia Borgia, became the master of a world, and then abandoned it for a desert of inner torment, anguish, spiritual struggle, trials, tortures and spies.

CHAPTER 5

At the Court of the Queen of Cyprus

Pietro's life was like a play performed on the stage of the greatest Italian courts of the age, as if a skilled stage director were standing in the wings throughout, skilfully pulling ropes to manoeuvre magnificent backdrops into place behind him. All the cradles of the Renaissance were represented — Venice, Ferrara, Urbino, Rome — and, for a while, the small village of Asolo in Veneto. Small, but famous thanks to a special prerogative: it played host to a real queen. Her presence within the borders of the Republic of Venice would not have been tolerated but for the fact that she was a queen in exile, a sovereign without a kingdom, honoured and revered only for the sake of appearances. Born Caterina Cornaro, she was a member of the Corner family, which claimed to descend in direct line from the ancient noble Roman family of Corneli. She married the King of Cyprus, Jacques de Lusignan, who died young, in 1473, when she was pregnant with their son. The Republic of Venice, keen to establish trade relations with that part of the Mediterranean, solemnly declared the widowed queen its adopted daughter and took her under its protection. After the death of Caterina's son, the boy king James III, Jacques de Lusignan's half-sister entered into an alliance with Ferdinand of Aragon, the King of Naples, in an attempt to regain the throne usurped from her by Lusignan. The pope gave the conspirators his blessing and several murderous intrigues ensued. After the state of emergency was resolved, and the island was again pacified, the Republic sent representatives to support Caterina, though this amounted in effect to removing her from power. Meanwhile, the island had become the target of new plots fomented by the sultans of Constantinople and Cairo. The Republic could no longer afford to temporise: in January 1489, Caterina's brother Andrea Corner was dispatched to Cyprus to persuade her to return to Venice, leaving the government of the island in the hands of the Venetian diplomats. She was to receive the court of Asolo and the title 'rejna de Jerusalem, Cypri et Armeniæ'.

Thanks to Pietro, we are able to stroll through her small court and explore its countless charming nooks and crannies on the occasion of a party organised by the queen for the wedding of one of her ladies-in-waiting, to which many noble ladies and gentlemen have been invited. Our attention is first drawn to the woods and houses huddled around the castle with a massive square tower surmounted by a loggia:

> The fair and pleasant castle of Asolo, built in the foothills of our mountains overlooking the marches of Treviso, belongs, as everyone should know, to my lady the Queen of Cyprus (with her family, which goes by the name of Cornelia and is much honored in our city of Venice, my own is joined by blood as well as friendship and familiarity).

In the above passage, which appears in the *incipit* of the final version of *Gli Asolani* [Figure 16], Pietro depicts Asolo as a paradise on earth, but says nothing about the circumstances surrounding the queen's exile. The original draft, however, was quite different:

> The fair and pleasant castle of Asolo, my lady, built in the foothills of our mountains overlooking the marches of Treviso, belongs (as you most certainly know) to the Queen of Cyprus, who, after the death of her late husband King James, having remained in a state of childless widowhood until long past her youth, to the satisfaction of her entire people left her kingdom in the hands of our Signoria and returned to her native Venice to see her parents and spend the remaining years of her life in her homeland, close to her family. She was warmly welcomed by her relatives and received many valuable gifts from the Signoria, including this castle, which I find pleasant and agreeable above all others due to its situation, the surrounding countryside and its healthy air.

In his final version, Pietro opted to remove everything that might detract from the idyllic atmosphere of the dialogue the reader is about to discover. If one wishes to know what Asolo might have looked like to Caterina's guests, one need only loose oneself in the depths of Lorenzo Lotto's *Pala di Asolo*, painted in 1506, the year following the publication of *Gli Asolani* [Figure 17]. It depicts the apparition of the Virgin between St Anthony and St Ludovic of Toulouse, amidst a rocky landscape painted in earthen hues, sparsely planted with trees and bisected by a river, which forms a small pool in the foreground. The houses, barns and mill in the distance have high thatched roofs in the northern style. The fortress of Asolo, with its unusually shaped tower, stands at the top of a forested hill, which today is entirely built up. The Virgin has the same full, slightly puffy and dour traits as Caterina in her portrait by Gentile Bellini [Figure 18].

Now, let us return to the wedding. Pietro vividly describes the view we would see if we were standing on the palace balcony alongside the group of three young men and three young women:

> This garden was of surpassing charm and beauty: in addition to a fair pergola of vines whose broad and shady structure divided it in the middle like a cross, a long and spacious walk, which was bestrewed with shining flint and might be entered at various places, ran around the perimeter. Except where there was an opening into the pergola, this alley was fenced on its inner side by a hedge of very thick, green junipers whose tops might have reached the breast of one who had approached them in order to enjoy the scene, which was equally agreeable in every part. Along the outer edge time-honored laurels, standing much taller than the junipers and half-overarching the pathway with their upper boughs, grew so close and neatly pruned that not one leaf appeared to desire any place but that assigned to it; nor did they reveal any part of the wall behind them except, at either end of one side, the milk-white marble of two ample windows.

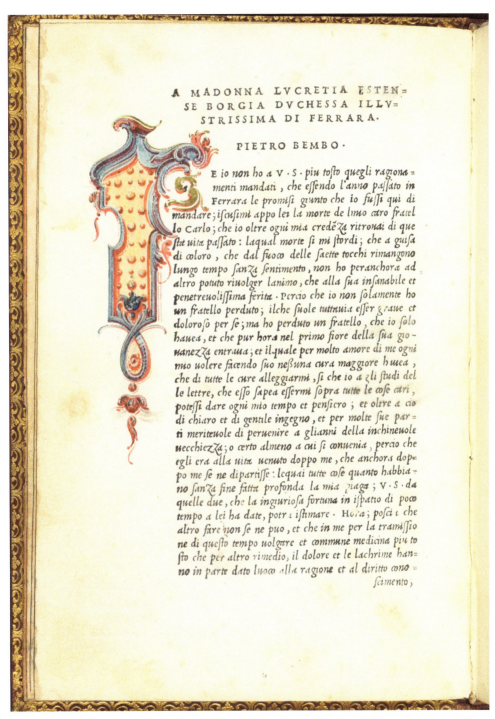

Fig. 16. Pietro Bembo, *Gli Asolani di Messer Pietro Bembo*, Venice, Aldus, 1505, f. 1 r°. First edition. Fondation Barbier-Mueller pour l'étude de la poésie italienne de la Renaissance, University of Geneva. Photo: Fondation Barbier-Mueller pour l'étude de la poésie italienne de la Renaissance, University of Geneva

Fig. 17. Lorenzo Lotto, *Assumption of the Virgin*, 1506, oil on wood, 175 × 162 cm, Duomo, Asolo. © Electa/Leemage

Fig. 18. Gentile Bellini, *Caterina Cornaro, Queen of Cyprus*, c. 1500, tempera on canvas, 63 × 49 cm, Szepmueveszeti Muzeum, Budapest. Foto: Razso Andras © 2015. The Museum of Fine Arts Budapest/Scala, Florence

That charming garden contains a holy of holies, a place in which human artifice has attained such a degree of perfection that it seems perfectly spontaneous, prefiguring the 'art of dissimulating art', which Baldassarre Castiglione called *sprezzatura* and considered an essential attribute of the perfect courtier:

> a little glade of tender grass, all carpeted with many sorts of charming flowers. Beyond this, the laurels, which here grew lawlessly in greater quantity than elsewhere, formed two groves of equal size, black with shade and reverent in their solitude; and deep between them harbored a delightful fountain, carved with consummate art out of the living rock with which the mountain closed the garden on this side. A little stream of clear, fresh water, gushing from the slope, fell into the fountain and from that, which stood at no great height above the earth, descended with a gentle sound into a miniature canal of marble which divided the glade; there received, murmuring and almost in hidden in the grass, it hurried on into the garden.

This is where three young men and three young women have agreed to meet to discuss love and recite poetry.

Following the technique of the humanistic dialogue, Pietro chose to address the same question from opposing points of view. Often, dialogues of this kind reached no real conclusion. But Pietro seems to have found an anchor point, by introducing a fourth male character, the hermit, which allowed him to reconcile the Neoplatonic perspective that permeates the dialogue with a Christian point of view. The two first protagonists, Perottino and Gismondo, present the sorrow and joy of love respectively. These two characters are in fact autobiographical masks of Pietro. The author never intervenes directly in the dialogue, but hovers over it like a spectre, beginning with a passage in the introduction that mentions his connection with the Cornaro family. Perottino was one of Pietro's nicknames (and coincidentally also the name of the servant who fathered a child with the seventeen-year-old Lucrezia Borgia in Rome), and Gismondo is twenty-six, the same age as Pietro when he started *Gli Asolani*. Moreover, and as we have seen, Pietro had recently pursued two complicated love affairs and was beginning a third with Lucrezia, to whom he later dedicated the dialogue (the dedicatory letter was not included in all copies of the first edition, suggesting some initial hesitation). If one searches carefully among the laurels and junipers in the garden, a complex web of allusions appears. Bernardo Bembo's device was a crown of laurels and palm fronds encircling a sprig of juniper; that design appears on the reverse side of Leonardo da Vinci's portrait of Ginevra Benci, commissioned, as noted earlier, by Bernardo; juniper bushes — an allusion to Ginevra's name — appear in her portrait as well. The queen's garden in *Gli Asolani* thus conjures up a familial memory in connection to the platonic love between Bernardo and Ginevra in Florence at the time of Lorenzo il Magnifico.

The two first days are devoted to a discussion of the cruelty and charms of love. However, Perottino and Gismondo are incapable of transcending a sensual, earthly view of love, and consequently they can present only an incomplete image of it, albeit one that is noble and exclusive. Is there a way out of this impasse? From personal experience, we know that both Perottino and Gismondo are right, depending on the circumstances. Pietro knew it too. At this point, he summons the experienced voice of the third gentleman, Lavinello, who attempts to solve the problem in the presence of the queen. Love is a desire given to us by nature, he argues, and as such, it is just, but only if one directs it toward a worthy and appropriate object. That object is beauty, which, in turn, consists of harmony and proportion: we are clearly in a Platonic view of love. But how does one attain beauty, if not with the eyes, ears and spirit? Of course, one should reject 'ugly things', which vulgar people often confuse with love. Lavinello thus associates love with the desire for beauty, which in turn tends to coincide with the idea of goodness; love is therefore fundamentally rational. It also involves the senses, since it relies on sight and hearing. In this way, we circle back to apparent beauty.

The answer to that quandary emerges unexpectedly from the dark depths of a forest spreading over a 'charming mountaintop'. Lavinello recounts how he entered the grove and found there a 'hut' inhabited by a 'bearded, white-haired man' dressed in clothes as rough as the bark of an oak. He is a holy hermit who lives frugally on a diet of grasses, roots, berries and water. Though the hermit was probably intended as a topical portrait, he may also allude to two of Pietro's friends, Tommaso Giustiniani and Vincenzo Querini, who around that time become hermits and tried to persuade Pietro to join them. Just as the hermit Paul, in the *Lives of the Fathers*, at once miraculously recognises St Anthony, the old man calls Lavinello by name from the moment he sees him. He then begins a long discourse on authentic love, reminding him that 'virtuous love is not merely desire of beauty, as you believe, but desire of true beauty, which is not of that human and mortal kind which fades, but is immortal and divine.' Corporeal beauty is but a miserable shadow of true beauty, which is divine and eternal. Man should guard against the testimony of his senses, since they draw him closer to his animal nature, when he should strive instead to approach incorruptible beauty, 'In order that our good genius may not grow angry with us and abandon us to our evil one when he sees that we bear more love to the surface of one little face and to these wretched and deceitful charms than to that mighty splendor whose ray is called the sun or to its true and everlasting beauties.'

Because he has free will, man is free to choose the object of his love: he can choose to lower himself to the state of an animal or rise to the angelic plane. This argument uncovers the influence of Pico de la Mirandola's *De hominis dignitate*, according to which man's ability to choose his own destiny gives him a singular role to play in the universe. The love discussed by Perottino and Gismondo is false, but no less so than the one presented by Lavinello, who occupies an intermediate position, in that he refuses to choose between sensual and heavenly love. Only by admiring the glory of nature is man driven to contemplate absolute beauty, the divine harmony that never fades nor deteriorates. He reminds Lavinello that there is

> another world which is neither material nor evident to sense, but completely separate from this and pure; a world which turns around this one and is both sought and found by it [...] a world divine, intelligent and full of light [...] and in which the grass is never brown, the plants are never withered, the creatures never die, the seas are never rough, the air is never dark, the fire never parches, nor must its heavens and their bodies turn continually.

In that authentic world, or *locus amœnus*, symbolised by the queen's garden, with its clear water, green grass, flowers and luxuriant vegetation, love is embodied in its truest, most eternal and perfect form.

In Asolo, by contrast, love was fleeting; perfect one moment, disappearing the next, it had to be laid down in words that could stand the test of time. To that end, Pietro constantly honed his prose — but also, more importantly, his verse — by purging it of any contingent and artificial elements introduced by current events or fashions. A strict adherence to the style of Petrarch further contributed to shaping the concept and projecting it across the centuries. This explains not only his decision to expunge all references to Caterina's past, but also his increasingly terse and simple poetic style, which contains none of the romantic or narrative elements and realistic scenes of everyday life common in late-gothic literature. Pietro, like Michelangelo after him, proceeded by elimination, producing unadorned, crystal-clear forms as a way of focusing our attention on the essential. But he enveloped those forms in lightness and musical grace, qualities he would later recognise in the faces painted by his friend Raphael.

The hermit has some harsh words for Lavinello, but then proceeds to tell him a fascinating tale: the legend of the queen of the Fortunate Isles. The story may have been inspired by an actual event from 1497, the year Bembo started writing *Gli Asolani*. On 17 May 1497, the Venetian ambassador Francesco Cappello conveyed to Venice a gift from the royal family of Spain, in the form of the brother of a *cacique*, or native chief, brought back by Christopher Columbus from his second Atlantic crossing. The *cacique*, renamed Diego Colón, arrived in Padua, where he can still be seen in a fresco of the Wedding of the Virgin, by Giulio Campagnola, in Scoletta del Carmine. That event clearly made an impression on Pietro; in Book IV of his *Historia vinitiana*, he reported the arrival in Venice of the 'King of one of the Fortunate Isles [...] in the Atlantic Ocean, approximately a thousand miles from land to the South.' Thus, the story of the queen who wanted to be loved and adored while remaining forever a virgin contains elements of both history and myth.

The queen in the hermit's story rewards her would-be lovers according to the merits of their love. First, however, she tests them by tapping them with a small wand, which sends them to sleep as soon as they leave her palace. When they wake up, the image of their dreams is inscribed on their foreheads (another variation on the recurrent theme of inner life made visible). Those who dream of wild beasts, hunting, fishing or riding she sends to live among the animals of their dreams. Conversely, those who dream of remaining by her side are received with varying degrees of intimacy, depending on the intensity of the desire revealed by their dreams. However, a third group of dreamers is of special interest to us:

> Of those whose dreams had evidently been concerned with trade or governing their families and communities or similar things, yet little with the queen herself, she appointed one to be a merchant, one a citizen, one an elder in his city, weighing them down with heavy thoughts and taking no more care for them than they for her.

The figure of Bernardo Bembo in *De Ætna*, burdened with heavy worries and cares, looms over this quasi-Dantean interpretation of the *lex talionis*. What this passage also expresses clearly is Pietro's rejection of any form of *mercatantare* (haggling or bargaining). He explained this bluntly in a letter to his friend Bibbiena, dated 29 August 1505: 'I am completely incapable of conforming to that ambitious, mercantile lifestyle, nor do I wish to have any dealings with people who follow such a way of life. My heart is filled only with a desire to study, which delivers me from the ambition and haggling that are fashionable nowadays.'

The myth of the queen of the Fortunate Isles perfectly encapsulated the existential programme that Pietro decided to follow whole-heartedly from that moment on, by pursuing a career at court and staking his personal and literary reputation on the theme of love, especially virginal love, detailed in a style resembling the *dolce stilnovo*. That explains why Baldassarre Castiglione, in Book IV of *The Courtier*, gave Pietro the task of discussing the form of love most suitable for the perfect courtier (from a Neoplatonic perspective, though one more tolerant of love's sensual dimension). However, Pietro's programme implied a double rejection; on the one hand, of the conventions of late-medieval, courtly love, and, on the other, of the dominant ethical code of Venice, which is clearly targeted by the references to merchants, city elders and the governing of families in the preceding quotation. Pietro's dream was a dream of love, and it offered him an opportunity to grow close to the queens of many of the Fortunate Isles scattered across early sixteenth-century Italy. In the world of literature at least — for in life he was rather more likely to indulge the call of the flesh — Pietro emerged as the herald of a new courtly culture, one that was spiritual and aloof from sensual experience and revolved around a dialogue of love. By means of a vocabulary as purified and reproducible as Petrarch's, it quickly established a code of its own, one that was more social and behavioural than literary.

Pietro's main contribution to Renaissance culture thus consisted in shaping this new mindset. *Gli Asolani* functioned as a vast reservoir of subject matter for love poems. In this sense it was an almost meta-literary work; Gismondo reveals its true nature when he points out to Perottino that his lament repeats what love poetry has been saying for centuries. The traditional critique and praise of love are summarised on the two first days, after which they are filtered through the spiritual and vaguely mystical key of the hermit on the third. *Gli Asolani* then ends somewhat abruptly right after Lavinello's story, without any definitive conclusion or resolution. As noted above, the dialogue reflects a moment of unstable equilibrium, since its writing coincided with the progressive dissolution of a group of friends who were united by a common interest in poetry, games and conversation, as well as by the rules of transparent, disinterested friendship expressed by the *Leggi della Compagnia degli Amici*.

Tommaso Giustiniani and Vincenzo Querini planned to embrace the monastic calling and tried to persuade Pietro to join them. Their spiritual quest is reflected in a series of quasi-spiritual modifications to the draft of the *Leggi*, which, curiously, were not included in the revised and corrected version. Indeed, like *Gli Asolani*, the *Leggi* remained open to an unspecified number of revisions. As noted in the preceding chapter, each member was expected to have his portrait painted and inscribe his device on the back. The portraits would then be bound in a book, with the member's likeness on one side of the page and the device on the other. One imagines that *Gli Asolani* may have been intended to replace that book of portraits by presenting a series of idealised, spiritual portraits of the members of the *Compagnia*, just as Giorgione's *Ritratto Ludovisi* [Figure 19], a portrait of two of the *Amici*, illustrates the contrasting temperaments — melancholy and sensual — of Perottino and Gismondo in *Gli Asolani*.

Gli Asolani can also be seen as a likeness of Pietro: he is reflected in all the characters without being identified with any single one. More importantly, however, he had by then firmly decided to be a poet of love and a courtier. The spiritual worries that agitated the Amici, and led some of them to choose the life of a hermit, were, in Pietro's case, either resolved through literature or temporarily dismissed as one of many possible paths.

A geographical coincidence illustrates the very different directions chosen by the Amici. In 1506, Vincenzo Querini, a close friend of Pietro's, joined a monastery on the island of Murano, where he intended to study Hebrew and pursue spiritual renewal. He hoped his learned friend would eventually decide to join him. Many years later, in 1550, Giovan Francesco Straparola, a writer from Bergamo, published a fascinating collection of short stories in the style of folktales, *Le piacevoli notti*, the introduction to which places them around the mid-1530s:

> There lived in Milan, the capital of Lombardy, a city full of women, beautiful palaces and everything one might expect to find in such a glorious city, a man named Ottaviano Maria Sforza [...]. But the harshness of those times, the many ferocious hatreds and murderous struggles, and the incessant political turmoil, forced him to secretly flee to Lodi with his daughter Lucrezia, wife of Giovanfrancesco Gonzaga, cousin of Federico Marchese of Mantua. He stayed there for a while, but his relatives continued to persecute him. Despairing of his family's ruthlessness and hatred toward himself and his recently widowed daughter, the poor man took what little money and jewellery were left him and travelled to Venice. There, he was honourably received by Ferier Beltramo, a kind and gentle man of noble lineage. As living in another man's house as a guest soon grows uncomfortable, he quickly resolved to find a place to live. Accompanied by his daughter, he crossed by boat to Murano, where a very beautiful palace was available. Finding it pleasant, with a large courtyard, wonderful loggia and pretty garden overflowing with flowers, fruits and grasses, they decided to settle there. A marble staircase led up to a magnificent hall, several beautiful rooms and a balcony that overlooked the water, which was all around the island. [...] Many noble and learned gentlemen formed a good and honourable society, including Casal of Bologna, a bishop and ambassador of the King of England, the scholar Pietro Bembo, knight of the Great Master of Rhodes, and Vangelista Cittadini of Milan, a man of superior talent. These men made up the first circle around the mistress of the house. Also present were the great poet Bernardo Capello, the love-struck Antonio Bembo, the son of Venice Benedetto Trivigiano, the friendly Antonio Molino, nicknamed Burchiella, and the ceremonious Ferier Beltramo. [...] All, or a great number, of those gentlemen came almost every evening to Madame Lucrezia's house and entertained her with charming dances, brilliant talk, music and songs. And so, in this or that way, they whiled away the voluble and fleeting time.

It is possible that Straparola never met Pietro, although they both frequented the

Fig. 19. Giorgione, *Ritratto Ludovisi*, early sixteenth century, oil on canvas, 76.3 × 63.4 cm, Museo di Palazzo Venezia, Rome. © 2015. Photo Scala, Florence; courtesy of the Ministero Beni e Att. Culturali

house of their mutual friend Andrea Navagero in Murano around the same time; it is possible too that the soirées he described never actually took place. Yet it seems significant that the place to which Vincenzo withdrew to study the Bible provided an opportunity for Pietro to engage in courtly, learned conversation with pretty women and cultivated gentlemen, in the most charming setting — an almost perfect replica of *Gli Asolani*. In a sense, Straparola unwittingly marked the inevitable parting of the ways, when Pietro and the Amici started to move in very different directions.

CHAPTER 6

The Carnival of Venus

When the windows facing the high peak of Monte di Catri were opened, they saw that dawn was breaking in the east, lovely and pink, and all the stars had faded from the sky but Venus, that tender queen of the heavens, who marks the boundary between night and day. The day was dawning sweet and cold, while in the nearby hills the woods rang with a concert of birdsong.

A winter morning in Urbino. Duchess Elisabetta Gonzaga has spent the night in the Palazzo Ducale entertaining her guests with a fascinating discussion. For fun, she challenged the gentlemen she had invited to spend Carnival night at the palace, among whom was Pietro Bembo, to answer the following question: what qualities define the consummate courtier, the perfect *cortegiano*?

A fine day was rising over Urbino, but among those present there was a strong presentiment of darker days ahead. Duke Guidubaldo, the melancholy, delicate but courageous son of Federico, paragon of courtliness and learning, spent the entire night in his rooms. He had long suffered from numerous ailments, which would ultimately result in his death less than a year later. As Baldassarre Castiglione would later write to the English King Henry VIII, his demise plunged Urbino into the icy gloom of a futureless eclipse: on the night of his death and for the next few days 'the stars [...] grew dim [...] and everything in Nature reeked of death and horror.'

Guidubaldo was a prodigy, endowed with a remarkable memory and exceptionally knowledgeable on many subjects. As the son of General Federico da Montefeltro, he would most certainly have accomplished great things had he not suffered from gout from a young age. Born in 1472, he succeeded his father at the tender age of ten. It was a time of great unrest, and the duchy was caught in a stranglehold between Rome, Venice and Florence. To make matters worse, its coffers were empty; the building of a magnificent palace and a library filled with the finest manuscripts — Federico disdained print — most of them on parchment, had dealt the duchy's finances a mortal blow. In 1502, around the time when Pietro was romancing Lucrezia Borgia, the latter's brother Cesare, 'the Valentino', with the help of his father, Pope Alexander VI, attacked Urbino by treachery. The duke and duchess were forced to flee to Venice, where Pietro first met them. Guidubaldo later regained control of his duchy and enjoyed several years of relative peace, during which Urbino confirmed its reputation as one of the most brilliant courts in Italy. Just as Piero della Francesca, Francesco di Giorgio Martini and Luciano Laurana had made the reputation of Federico's court, under his son's reign, all the great poets writing in the vernacular flocked to Urbino and dedicated their books to Elisabetta. Time passed peacefully in Urbino amidst plays, learned conversation and games of all kind.

Disillusioned at the failure of his political ambitions in Venice, Pietro decided to play his final hand at the court of Rome. In the summer of 1506, he set off for the papal city, intending to stop along the way in Urbino. The stopover — which lasted six years — allowed him to further cultivate his Humanist interests and, more importantly, to familiarise himself with vernacular lyrical love poetry. During this time in Urbino, he also added to his repertoire verses of a lighter, more sensual, at times licentious nature such as the *Motti*, as well as carnivalesque yet refined compositions such as the *Stanze*, and more severe, solemn works such as the poem commemorating the death of his brother Carlo. He continued to work on his *Prose della volgar lingua*, and completed the first half by the end of his stay.

Arriving at the Mercatale plain below the slender towers of the Palazzo Ducale, urging his horse up the helical ramp designed by Francesco di Giorgio Martini, Pietro could hardly have imagined how eventful the next few years would be. History — both the small and personal and the solemn and official — continued its inexorable forward march. Everything was changing fast, maybe too fast. Pietro mourned the death of his much-loved brother Carlo in 1507, followed in 1508 by that of Guidubaldo and Cardinal Galeotto Della Rovere, his protector at the court of Pope Julius II. Around the same time, he began his career in the Curia and received his first ecclesiastical benefice, the Commenda dell'Ordine Gerosolimitano (Commandership of the Knights of St John of Jerusalem), although it came into effect only in 1517. It was the first in a long series of benefices, which reached a total of thirty by the end of his life and returned an estimated annual income of 1,665 ducats.

Meanwhile, the situation in Venice was growing increasingly dire. The year 1508 was especially problematic: the pope backed the League of Cambrai, hoping in this way to put a halt to Venice's expansion and divide its possessions among his allies in the League, who included Louis XII of France, Emperor Maximilian I, the Marquis of Mantua, the King of Naples and the Duke of Ferrara. The situation of Venice became progressively more critical; on 14 May 1509, the armies of the Serenissima were defeated at Agnadello. Venice lost almost all its territories on the mainland. Urbino was a traditional ally of Venice; its dukes held the rank of commander of the Venetian armies. The lion of St Mark visible today in the throne room of the ducal palace testifies to that connection.

Around the same time, Guidubaldo, who was sterile — a condition rumoured to be the result of dark arts practiced against him by his tutor Ottaviano Ubaldini, a cousin of his father's — adopted as his heir a nephew of the pope, Francesco Maria Della Rovere, a young man of violent disposition with little interest in scholarship (his mother was Federico's sister Giovanna da Montefeltro and his father was Giovanni Della Rovere, a nephew of Sixtus IV). Like his uncle Guidubaldo, Francesco married a Gonzaga, Eleonora. In less than two years, the atmosphere in Urbino underwent a radical transformation from the one that Pietro encountered in 1506 or earlier. The new duke and duchess had none of their predecessors' charisma.

Francesco Maria was a warrior first and foremost: he began his military career as a captain in the papal army and rose to prominence in the service of the Serenissima, becoming captain-general of the Venetian forces. He was closely linked to the Doge, Andrea Gritti, who was responsible for the spectacular architectural renovation that shaped the city as we know it today, his greatest achievement being the Piazza San Marco. Although Francesco's circle also included many intellectuals and patrons of the arts, he was a soldier at heart and saw art and beauty merely as a way of satisfying a 'momentary desire to escape the horrors of war'. For Pietro, Guidubaldo and Elisabetta's reign remained a dazzling memory, which he immortalised in a dialogue in 1509–10. His friend Baldassarre Castiglione also recalled the reign of Guidubaldo and Elisabetta with rapturous nostalgia in his *Cortegiano*. Their common friend Raphael painted the portraits of the ill-starred former duke and duchess, leaving the task of portraying their successors to Titian, who did so in 1536–37, in two famous paintings, which now hang in the Uffizi Gallery [Figures 20–21].

Pietro and Francesco Maria became friends and remained close long after Pietro's departure. Years later, when the duke and duchess decided to renovate the Villa Imperiale in Pesaro, they asked Pietro to provide several Latin inscriptions. The villa was intended as a relaxing retreat where the duke might rest after the rigours of the battlefield. Accordingly, Pietro's first inscription, 'Pro sole, pro pulvere, pro vigiliis, pro laboribus' ('In exchange for the sun, the dust, the vigils and the labours'), suggests that all the pleasant things in the villa — the meadows, springs, flowers and so on — exist to reward the Duke for suffering the discomforts of war. Pietro struck a similarly nostalgic and elegiac chord in the final lines of a letter to Giovan Jacopo Leonardi, orator of the Duke in Venice, in 1533: 'Please recommend me to the good graces of the Duke and Duchess, for I wish I could visit them in that beautiful country of theirs, which is so dear to my heart, and live under that sky again for eight days'. Pietro may have been thinking of himself as well when writing about the vigils, the dust and the labours faced by Francesco Maria.

Though not marked by any event of particular importance, Pietro's time in Urbino was one of intense authorial activity alternating with periods of spiritual retreat, especially to Fonte Avellana, the monastery where the hermit St Peter Damian (St Pier Damiani) withdrew several centuries earlier. There, he tried to reconnect with himself and restore his inner peace, which had been upset by his ambitions — but also his father's ambitions for him — his love affairs and the sirens of court life. The sonnet *Re degli altri superbo et sacro monte* is addressed to the mountain where the hermitage stood, and where he hoped to 'free myself from the unwholesome aspects of my desires'. In a letter to Elisabetta Gonzaga and Emilia Pio, on 3 May 1506, Bembo explained his need to withdraw from the world for extended periods. In this regard too, Petrarch was his model:

> Is not living in quietude and rest, free from worry and melancholy, the best use one can make of life? Especially when that quietude is complemented by an honourable activity such as writing, which yields its most precious and graceful fruits under circumstances such as these. The valorous Tuscan whom we all love and admire understood this well: of all the stages of his life, it was during the ten years of solitary retreat in La Sorgue that he found the greatest satisfaction and harvested the most beautiful fruits.

Fig. 20. Titian, *Portrait of Eleonora Gonzaga Della Rovere*, 1536–38, oil on canvas, 114 × 103 cm, Uffizi Gallery, Florence. Photo Scala, Florence; courtesy of the Ministero Beni e Att. Culturali

Fig. 21. Titian, *Portrait of Francesco Maria Della Rovere, Duke of Urbino*, 1536, oil on canvas, 114 × 103 cm, Uffizi Gallery, Florence. © 2015 Photo Scala, Florence; courtesy of the Ministero Beni e Att. Culturali

The same feeling is expressed even more clearly in a sonnet dedicated to Tommaso Giustiniani, a member of the *Compagnia degli Amici* who later became a religious reformer (*Thomaso, i'venni ove l'un duce mauro*). Tommaso received the poem just as he was preparing to leave for the Holy Land; like Pietro, he was abandoning Venice. Perhaps he hoped to find there the peace that his friend seemed finally to have achieved.

> Sometimes, when sitting on a green riverbank,
> and speaking or writing about my Lady,
> I turn my mind from other thoughts.
> Thus, with shy and solitary soul,
> I lead a peaceful and untroubled life,
> disdaining the world and of myself most of all.

The sentiment is reiterated in another sonnet from the Urbino period, *Hor c'ho le mie fatiche tante et gli anni*: 'Vain and deceptive world, I reject you | and repent for believing in you until now'.

Unsurprisingly, the Urbino poems are mostly addressed to friends, in accordance with the traditional game of courtly homages. Indeed, the court of Urbino remained on the sidelines of the major political struggles of the time, and therefore served as a meeting place for intellectuals from all over Italy, including Ludovico da Canossa of Verona, Baldassarre Castiglione, who hailed from Mantua, and the brothers Ottaviano and Federico Fregoso, who fled their homeland after the French invasion (Ottaviano eventually became Doge of Genoa and Federico a cardinal). Court life was gallant, and courtiers were very fond of games, like the one described in the sonnet *Io ardo, dissi, et la risposta in vano*. In this game, gentlemen and ladies sat in a row and the first in line whispered a sentence to the person seated next to him, who then whispered her response to the next person, and so on. At the end of the game, each player in turn said their sentence out loud, which resulted in a very strange composite text.

The above-mentioned sonnet gave rise to the rumour that Pietro was in love with Duchess Elisabetta:

> One evening, the courtiers decided to play the Sienese game *isproposito*, in which one person whispers something into his neighbour's ear, who must then whisper something to the person next to him and so on, until the end. On the evening when the game was played, Bembo was seated next to the duchess, for she often favoured him in this way. He whispered to her the words 'I burn'. She, however, did not answer 'so do I' or 'not I' or something of the kind, as he had hoped, but prudently chose words unrelated to his. For the next two days, Bembo was beside himself with disappointment. On the third evening, the game was played again, and Bembo was seated next to the duchess again. When it came to his turn, his words expressed none of the melancholy of his previous offering. The duchess very courteously stood up to console him: she rewarded him with a tender look and placed her hand on his as it rested on the arm of his chair. Her hand was cold, but Bembo was so elated that he failed to notice this fact. Later, however, he claimed that the duchess, by giving him her cold hand, intended to convey the coolness of her heart, and he wrote a sonnet about it. The sonnet implies that Bembo loved the duchess, but that she, though admiring his many virtuous qualities, could not in all honesty return his feelings.

The court of Urbino was a veritable literary laboratory. Almost all the poets of the late fifteenth-century courtly school either addressed poems to the duchess or dedicated books to her. Their poetry was often highly mannered and, linguistically speaking, bore the influence of various local or regional dialects; it was certainly less pure than Bembo's. Like late-gothic paintings, their poems are often witty, conceptual, anecdotic and full of lively little scenes. In the meantime, Pietro and Baldassarre Castiglione, with the help of Castiglione's cousin Cesare Gonzaga, were laying the foundations of a new kind of poetry. Some of their works stand as manifestos for a new classical trend: the texts are simpler and more structured, the language texturally close to Petrarch's, the themes less pedestrian and concrete. Their style grew more rarefied and spiritual, on the model of the style Pietro experimented with in *Gli Asolani*. One could argue that the limitations this placed on the registers, themes, metaphors and even words that could be used robbed the language and poetry of a some of its richness. But it was the necessary price to pay for a new model, which would soon impose itself all across Europe and would be viewed, by the early eighteenth century, after a century of baroque acrobatics, as a standard of rationality and balance.

In their verse, Pietro and his friends created a solar myth around the Urbino court, which served to obscure its slow decline. The dedicatory ballad introducing Pietro's collected poems praises Elisabetta's 'great and clear virtue [...] which is almost like a sun, outshining all other lights'. This image of the duchess echoes the portrait of the duke in *Tirsi*, a pastoral poem in *ottave* by Baldassarre Castiglione and Cesare Gonzaga, which recounts several events at the court of Urbino and describes Guidubaldo as 'learned and wise, a sun in our midst' (stanza LI). This poem transports the reader back to the Carnival of 1507. To mark the occasion, Venus sent two ambassadors to the hills of Montefeltro. Two rather strange ambassadors, it must be said: a future doge and a future cardinal. Ottaviano Fregoso and Pietro Bembo were charged with delivering the goddess's message, an invitation to appreciate love and savour the pleasures of mortal life, which so quickly fade and wither. Turning to Elisabetta, her cousin Emilia Pio and the court ladies, the ambassadors transmitted the words of the goddess of Cyprus (XXXI):

> Your beauty is like a garden
> and the years of your youth like its April and May,
> the season when our master, if he pleases,
> visits this land, bringing joy and happiness.
> But when the sun burns the flowers,
> or bitter frost blankets the countryside,
> without a care in the world, he waits
> in a cool place for the heat to subside,
> or warms himself by the fire in winter.

Enjoy youth and freshness while it lasts is the message of the *Stanze*, for, as the final poem unequivocal warns: 'Youth and beauty, when unused, are like hidden gems' (XXXII). The *Stanze*'s fifty eight-line poems exuberantly celebrate the joy of love, especially carnal love, which for once is not sublimated but referred to openly. Young women are urged to reject the absurd custom of chastity, and the myth of modesty and abstinence. Only the ignorant and superstitious masses, the weak-spirited, the fanatical and the bigoted still believe that love leads to sin and dishonour:

> The price of chastity, praised and worshipped
> by the ancients in prose and verse,
> and the ideas of sin and of dishonour
> that encumber stupid, errant folk [...]
> are but false romances, dreams and shadows
> which oppress and burden simpler souls. (XXXVI)

Furthermore, if carnal love were really such a terrible sin, would God and nature have made it so enjoyable? The *Stanze* recall the Carnival songs traditionally composed in Florence at the time of Lorenzo il Magnifico, the world that Pietro discovered as a young boy; they were in fact written during the Carnival season. The dominant mood, expressed in a style at once precious and popular, is one of festive rejoicing. In his dedication, dated Ash Wednesday 1507, Ottaviano Fregoso's explains the hurried circumstances of their composition (literally, they were 'warped' on a 'hasty loom'):

> The *Stanze* were warped by your Ladyship and woven by me with thread spun during those pleasant days, which, according to an ancient custom, are given over to rejoicing and licence, and intended to be performed as a masque before the Duchess and Madonna Emilia. [...] Whosoever shall hear or read them, if ever, can have no idea of how hastily they were composed, amid the dances and banquets and joyous clamour of that delightful time of year.

The *Stanze* were also a musical success: a number of versions with tablatures were published. Pietro reworked the text at several times, in particular for the first edition of his collected verse, the *Rime*, in 1530. Despite their occasional, courtly origin, they were never removed from the successive editions of the *Rime*. This indicates that the *Stanze* conformed more closely to Bembo's ideal of refined Petrarchan classicism than other poems, which were removed because of their association with the poetic universe of the fifteenth century. The *Stanze*, *Tirsi* and the beautiful song *Alma cortese, che dal mondo errante*, which Pietro composed in honour of his late brother Carlo in December 1507 (several years after his death on 31 December 1503), are the first signs of a stylistic transformation, which would be definitively codified only two decades later.

Alma cortese and the *Stanze* are a study in contrasts. The *Stanze* are an invitation to relish life, bursting with carnival joy and subtle yet explicit allusions to sensuality, whereas the song is grave and solemn. The beloved brother plucked from life in the flower of youth had been a friend to Pietro, a confidante, a safe haven, a refuge from his passions and hopes, a source of pleasure: 'in your presence, rage and worry disappear, like shadows vanishing in the presence of the sun'. In Pietro's imagination, Carlo's heart was also made of crystal:

> Never did glass reflect these colours,
> perse, white or vermillion,
> nor pure spring reveal its grassy bed

> as clearly as in your eyes I read
> all my desires and doubts reflected.

In Urbino, Bembo experimented with two contrasting aspects of his poetry. The first, and dominant, one was aristocratic. The second, dictated by necessity, adopted a more popular style, but was never developed to its full potential. A rare example of the latter type survives in the form of a relatively unknown but highly significant work, the *Motti*, which was written around the carnival period of 1507. It consists in a series of couplets in hendecasyllables, designed to be used in one of the many games of chance played at court. The aim of the game was to combine different couplets — proverbs, riddles or *centoni* (combinations of lines from works by famous authors such as Virgil, Dante or Petrarch) — into questions and answers by following certain rules or rolling the dice. The *Motti* are full of erudite references to mythology and licentious or obscene innuendo. The combination of the theme of love and the strangeness of the chance pairings of questions and answers heightened the players' enjoyment of the poetry. For once, that poetry could also be an object of mockery, by parodying a famous verse of Virgil's third eclogue, for instance, or slyly slipping in a false Petrarchan couplet, or gently ridiculing the poet of Arezzo's verses by presenting them as proverbs. Probably the most surprising feature of this work for the modern reader is the series of obscene riddles towards the end of the book, which seem like the work of a poet much less accomplished than Bembo:

> What is always swaddled in clothing and goes hungry if it doesn't throw up its meal?
> What is always tossing and turning, and spills blood without cutting a vein?
> And who is that gentleman with two dogs that never follow him into the garden?
> And tell me where is the cave that only the blind can enter?
> And where is the valley that blooms red every month?
> And where in that valley flows the spring from which one can drink only after drilling the mountain?

How Emilia and Elisabetta must have blushed when these riddles reached their chaste ears!

In fact, that popular and openly pornographic vein in poetry was nothing new. It even achieved a certain level of dignity and legitimacy about twenty years later, in Rome, under Clement VII, thanks to Pietro Aretino. The popularity of the genre grew exponentially from that point onward, inspiring scores of burlesque poems full of unrepeatable sexual innuendo, which were composed for the most part between the 1520s and 1540s. Pietro had dabbled in the genre, especially in his Latin poems, which explored erotic themes, albeit in a different and far more refined way. The most striking example is the poem *Priapus*, in which the god of gardens and fertility sings the praises of the most beautiful plant in his garden, which can be used in many ways to satisfy unhappy women. At the end of the poem, an imaginary interlocutor asks Priapus what this plant is called. The mystery is soon resolved: its name is *menta pusilla* ('little mint', the diminutive of which is *mentula*, a synonym of penis). The poem may have been inspired by the daring woodcut of the triumph of

HYEMI AEOLIAE.S.

Ad questo nobile figmento el præstante artifice, electo solertemente el marmoro haueua, che oltra la candidecia sua era uenato (al requisito loco) de nigro, ad exprimere el tenebroso aere illumino, & nebuloso cum cadente grandine. Sopra la plana della dicta ueneranda, Ara rigidamente rigoroso, pmineua el rude simulachro del hortulano custode, cum tutti gli sui decenti & propriati insignii. Laquale mysteriosa Ara tegeua uno cupulato umbraculo, sopra quatro pali nel solo infixi affirmato & substentato. Gli quali pali diligentemente erano inuestiti di fructea, & florea frondatura, Et el culmo tutto intecto de multiplici fiori, & tra ciascuno palo nel lymbo dellapertura, o uero hiato del umbraculo affixo pendeua una ardente lampada, & in circuito ornatamente bracteedoro dalle fresche & uerifere aure inconstante uexate, & cum metallei crepituli sonante. nelquale simulachro, cum maxima religione & prisco rito rurale & pastorale alcune amole, o uero ampulle uitree cum spumáte cruore del immolato Asello, & cum caldo lacte & scintillante Mero spargendo rumpeuano, & cum fructi. fiori. fronde. festa, & gioie libauano, Hora drieto a questo glorioso Triumpho, conduceuano, cum antiqua & siluatica cerimonia illaqueato el seniculo Iano, de reste & trece intorte di multiplici fiori, cantanti carmini ruralméte Talassii, Hymænei, & Fescennii, & istrumenti rurestricum suprema lætitia & gloria, celebremente exultanti, & cum solenni plausi saltanti, & uoce fœmelle altisone, Per laquale cosa nó manco piacere & dilecto cum stupore quiui tali solenni riti & celebre feste me inuase, che la admiratione de gli præcedenti triumphi.
*

Fig. 22. [*Triumph of Priapus*], in Francesco Colonna, *Hypnerotomachia Poliphili*, Venice, Aldus, 1499, f. 98 r°. First edition. Fondation Martin Bodmer, Cologny, Geneva (Inc. B. 77). Fondation Martin Bodmer, Cologny, Geneva

Priapus illustrating the *Hypnerotomachia Poliphili* [Figure 22]; it certainly conjures up a similar atmosphere of audacious cultural experimentation deeply rooted in classical culture. Latin poetry gave authors a certain latitude to explore a greater diversity of themes than the vernacular, and eroticism was a central feature of it. Scenes of male homosexual love appear in another of Pietro's poems, in which a faun complains of being excluded from the games of a group of depraved, lascivious youths and their friends, the nymphs (*Faunus ad Nympeum fluvium*). Bembo also celebrated adulterous love, for instance in the poem *De amica a viro servata diligentissime* about two lovers living in the same building. The woman rises naked every morning to offer herself to her lover's gaze, but the two can never meet, because her husband watches her too closely. In a jealous rage, he even throws into the Adriatic Sea a ring his wife received from her lover and burns a jacket she is sewing for him. The husband is a stock character from comedy; he hides his sparse hair under a wig, sweetens his foul breath with jasmine and stubbornly refuses to realise that his wife would sin less if he left her free to sin! Like the *Stanze*, Bembo's polished Latin verses urge one to delight in the pleasures of love and reject hypocritical notions of modesty and abstinence.

Guidubaldo's death changed everything, as we have seen. Pietro wanted to take leave of the ducal couple in a way commensurate with the depth of his affection. He conceived a farewell tribute in two parts, the first of which would be a collection of poems dedicated to Elisabetta. The original manuscript, with Pietro's autograph corrections (now in the Biblioteca Marciana in Venice, Marc. It. IX 143), was compiled between late 1510 and March 1511, and includes sixty poems. It played an important role in the development of Italian lyrical poetry, by laying the foundations of the new Petrarchan orthodoxy. The poems in this collection use relatively few different metres, and show a distinct preference for the sonnet over other forms commonly found in fifteenth-century lyrical verse. The language, though not yet the perfectly regular Italian of the *Prose*, clearly aims to emulate Petrarch.

The second part of Bembo's valedictory was a dialogue, *De Urbini ducibus*, designed as a monument to the memory of Guidubaldo and Elisabetta. At the same time, it foreshadowed the next stage of the future cardinal's life: like a two-faced Janus, the dialogue looks simultaneously back to Venice and the unforgettable past, and forwards to Rome and a future full of promise. Guidubaldo's life history allowed Pietro to reconnect the many strands of his own life. The dialogue begins with a description of the sorrow caused in Venice by the news of the duke's death. The most incredulous and grief-stricken of all is Pietro's father Bernardo. Guidubaldo and Elisabetta Gonzaga had fled together to Venice after being expelled from their duchy by Valentino (though it would be more accurate to say that they reunited in Venice, since Elisabetta was in Ferrara at the time of the invasion as part of Lucrezia's entourage on the occasion of her wedding with Alfonso I d'Este). Bernardo, Elisabetta, Lucrezia: these three names evoke the carefree years of the *Compagnia degli Amici* (the dialogue was in fact dedicated to one of the *Amici*, Niccolò Tiepolo).

Pietro proceeded to construct a play of mirrors around the duke's death. He described how he walked with his friends Filippo Beroaldo il Giovane and Jacopo

Sadoleto to the Vatican to see the papal official Sigismondo de' Conti, a Humanist who wrote elegant Latin. Together, they read the letters recounting the duke's final moments, which had been sent from Urbino to Pope Julius II by Federico Fregoso, as well as the funeral oration given in the Duomo by Guidubaldo's tutor, Lodovico Odasi.

That story within the story illustrates the obsession with style of the future secretary *ai Brevi*. At one point, Bembo affirms his deep respect for Sigismondo's culture; at another, he asks Beroaldo what he thinks of Fregoso's epistolary style. In fact, Pietro completely rewrote Odasi's speech, transforming it into a highly sophisticated dialogue on the theme of the perfect prince, which aims to demonstrate Guidubaldo's superiority over examples from Antiquity. From an early age, he trained in the masculine and military arts and, though often unwell, he mastered them perfectly. He outshone all the Italian princes with his beauty and charm. His physical and military prowess was complemented by his vast erudition, which was not erudition for its own sake so much as the broad learning expected of a prince at the time. The art of eloquence, history and geography held no secrets for him. He was exceptionally skilled in medicine and, thanks to his prodigious memory, which allowed him to remember everything he learned, he had an astonishingly accurate recollection of classical poetry. He also exemplified two essential princely virtues, clemency and, especially, liberality, that is, the capacity to use the riches that fate had bestowed on him with fairness, as was expected of a good monarch. Discernible between the lines of Bembo's version of Odasi's speech is a vitriolic attack against the powerful princes of Italy, whose absence of virtue was the root cause of Italy's misfortunes:

> Most princes make poor use of their fortune; they believe that their happiness depends upon it, and that they can exercise power as they manage their appetites, and thus obtain everything they want. Consequently, there can be nothing chaste, honest, holy or safe in them: they are entirely corrupt and dissolute, deformed by fickleness, unbridled passion, crime, theft and rape. The princes who take the greatest care and effort in satisfying their appetites enjoy the widest following and highest esteem, and their houses are full of brazen, corrupt men, who have never known God's law and possess no shred of piety, reticence or respect. Our duke, dear citizens, was nothing like those princes: an honest spirit and honest heart, he always showed himself to be full of compassion, modesty and respect.

But in their jealousy, the gods exacted a high price. Guidubaldo was unable to sire a direct, legitimate heir. Bembo devised a spiritual explanation for this situation: the gods decided to extinguish Guidubaldo's line rather than give him an heir who could never equal him in virtue. But he seemed to hesitate when confronted with the illness that caused the duke such intense suffering, as if unable to find the words, before uttering a muted cry of protest against an unjust God:

> God granted him too short a life, and the best and most noble part of his brief existence was disfigured to the point that, in the end, the only faculties he retained were breathing and opening his eyes. [...] Moreover, so that he might feel that condition of pain more acutely, his life was so short and fleeting that

he might as well not have lived at all. For most of that time, he was like a dead man among the living.

Through a skilfully assembled series of testimonies, the dialogue depicts a life that was both unhappy and exemplary. Though certainly idealised, Pietro's account is always solidly anchored in affectionate remembrance and does not evade embarrassing details such as Guidubaldo's impotence or Elisabetta's enforced chastity. Consequently, the portrait of the ideal prince that emerges from the dialogue is especially credible. Urbino was undoubtedly unique; there — and there only — was the ideal of the perfect prince fully embodied. If he had lived longer, Guidubaldo might have emerged as the only Italian prince capable of leading the country out of the morass. But this wonderful phoenix, this Dantesque scented panther, whom scholars had followed and would continue to follow, spent most of his brief life among Urbino's narrow lanes, red-brick houses and steep staircases opening onto breath-taking views of the viridian hills of Montefeltro. Here he is again, in the poignant words of his tutor, filtered by his Venetian friend:

> You were the most just, benevolent and generous of men, endowed with unusual moderation, honesty, devotion, piety, faith and staunchness, but also extraordinary humanity, majesty, prudence and wisdom. You were blessed with the gift of forgetting both the offences you suffered and the advantages you granted. You were not haughty when the situation favoured you, nor weak when it did not. You endured bad luck, illness and, finally, death, with an equal countenance and even demeanour. When men of the future speak about you, they will say that you were the phoenix your mother saw in a dream, a man who will remain forever peerless, whose spiritual accomplishments and virtues will ensure he rises to the most fiery regions of the sky — that is, immortality — after his body is dead and buried.

Pietro's solemn and dignified elegy reflects the duke's beauty, virtue and constancy in the face of illness, misfortune and death. There is something of a mirror effect in the intertwining of personal and historiographical elements in this speech. Both Pietro and Guidubaldo had domineering fathers and, whether by choice or by fate, were prevented from leading a *vita activa*. For both men, the decision to pursue Humanist learning on an encyclopaedic scale was motivated not only by an innate passion for knowledge but also by a need to define a domain that was entirely their own. That may explain why, aside from the gratitude and affection he undoubtedly felt for the duke and duchess, Pietro was so determined to perpetuate the memory of Guidubaldo and immortalise his short stay on earth. According to Pietro's fictionalised account, Sigismondo de' Conti intended to write the tribute himself, but found himself overwhelmed by his many obligations and buried under a 'mountains of letters to write'.

Meanwhile, the much younger Pietro was trembling with excitement at the thought of burying himself in those very same mountains some time soon. First, however, he needed to give the story of his beloved protectors a suitable conclusion. After finishing the dialogue, Pietro translated it into Italian and dedicated it to the duchess (ms. Urbinate Latino 1030 Vatican Library). Finally, in early 1512, he heeded the siren-call of Rome.

CHAPTER 7

Roman Sensualities

Just as Pietro was preparing to leave Urbino, a man who had joined Pope Julius II's unsuccessful campaign against the Duke of Ferrara was travelling to Venice to tend to various affairs and business interests. He needed to find himself a second wife, among other things. He had just turned forty-five, in 1511, and time flew swiftly. He had his sights set on Margherita, the illegitimate daughter of Duke Federico of Mantua. But negotiations were moving slowly, when, all of a sudden, fate upset his best-laid plans.

Francesca Ordeaschi was breathtakingly beautiful. So beautiful, in fact, that the man refused to be parted from her. He decided to bring her with him to Rome. With his characteristic determination, he immediately took the necessary steps, prudently hiding Francesca in a convent for some time, before installing her in his villa on the banks of the Tiber, which he was in the process of turning into a veritable pleasure palace with the help of two of the city's most famous artists, Sebastiano del Piombo and Baldassarre Peruzzi. Their patron wanted the best — and he could afford it. And the best at that time was Raphael.

The man in question was Agostino Chigi, the richest man alive. His villa, known today as the Villa Farnesina, was a paean to love and sensuality; it combined an architectural scheme based on the principles of Vitruvius with an intellectually ambitious decorative scheme inspired by Ovid's *Metamorphoses*. To immortalise this love, which audaciously vaulted class barriers, Raphael opted for an image that was simultaneously highly idealised and poetic, but also sensual and carnal — as poetic and carnal as the middle-aged banker's passion for a very young and beautiful woman. Only the ancient pagan world could provide such an image. Raphael found it in Ovid. Sebastiano del Piombo had started work on a fresco on the mythical theme of the Cyclops Polyphemus who fell in love with the beautiful nymph Galatea. Spurning his love, the nymph burned with passion for the young Acis. Wild with jealousy, Polyphemus crushed Acis under the rock of Etna. The unfortunate youth was then transformed into a river god. This aquatic myth inspired Raphael to paint the magnificent fresco known as the *Triumph of Galatea* [Figure 23].

The goddess appears riding on a huge clamshell with paddles on its sides, while all around her mythological sea-creatures proclaim the triumph of sensuality. She seems strangely alone in her nudity — exposed, sensual and sculptural yet chaste. The figure achieves miraculous balance between modesty and passionate glorification of love. As if to emphasise the contrast, Raphael gave Galatea the appearance

Fig. 23. Raphael, *Triumph of Galatea*, 1511–12, fresco, Villa Farnesina, Rome. © 2015. Photo Scala, Florence

Fig. 24. Raphael, *St Catherine of Alexandria*, c. 1507, oil on wood, 71 × 55 cm, National Gallery, London. © 2015. Copyright The National Gallery, London/Scala, Florence

and, significantly, the upturned gaze of his *Saint Catherine of Alexandria*, which now hangs in the National Gallery in London [Figure 24].

Thus 'released from archaeological coldness', the figure of Galatea expresses 'a love that for the first time declared itself as fully aware of its carnality and rejoicing in it'. Pietro was fascinated by Galatea and the nymphs that populated the ancient imagination, with their generous breasts and fragrant bodies veiled in a sheer film of ocean foam. He imagined them engaging in lascivious play and eluding the powerful virility of fauns and satyrs. In a poem inspired by the Galatea myth, he described how, after the tragic episode of Polyphemus and Acis, the nymph is captured by a faun. She manages to escape from his clutches, but the faun almost drowns in pursuing her. Rising above the water, her breasts grazing the waves and her feet resting on the sea foam, she then mocks her foolish, primitive lover.

That was what Pietro hoped to find in Rome. Traces of the ancient world were visible everywhere, and artists were breathing new life into that legacy. As in Raphael's fresco, emulation was rapidly replacing imitation; artists absorbed the ancient models and incorporated them into new works infused with the spirit of Antiquity. The aim was no longer to turn out pale imitations, studies or erudite variations on a theme, but rather to breathe new life into art by drawing on the accumulated knowledge of the preceding centuries, and to create works that rivalled the masterpieces of the ancient Greeks and Romans. This is the idea underlying Pietro's dispute on imitation with Giovan Francesco Pico della Mirandola, mentioned earlier. But imitation was only one side of the argument; the other was the need for a language that was elegant, clear, easy to understand, regular and restrained. A language, in other words, that was classical in every sense of the term and left no room for extravagance and arbitrariness. Whether that language was deployed in the context of literature, architecture, sculpture or even official correspondence — such as the papal briefs that Pietro started to write in 1513 in his role as *segretario ai brevi* — was irrelevant. Such a language would allow Julius II, and more importantly his successor Leo X, to reaffirm the dignity of the Church and consolidate its cultural and spiritual supremacy.

That programme is clearly laid out in a series of Raphael's cartoons for tapestries to be woven by Flemish craftsmen. The figures, though powerfully muscular, are devoid of superfluous anatomical detail and arranged in an orderly, symmetrical and harmonious manner in front of actual monuments of ancient Rome, which both frame the scene and give it rhythm. The non-frontal disposition of the figures creates a pleasant sense of graceful, dignified movement. Furthermore, the measured variation, harmony and nobility of the cartoons, as well as the inclusion of ancient architectural and sculptural motifs, were chosen to meet specific rhetorical requirements. In brief, they encapsulated the apogee of Renaissance classicism. Raphael, like other contemporary painters — especially Leonardo da Vinci — who were starting to soften the rigid and artificially geometrical perspective of fifteenth-century art by studying the effect of air and light on figures, avoided all forms of rigidity, thereby putting into practice Castiglione's much-quoted idea of 'sprezzatura': an artifice so perfect as to appear natural.

Since the reign of Alexander VI, Rome was in effervescence. Everywhere ancient edifices were being excavated, classified and sketched. At the same time, others were being torn down, especially if they had been built during the much-reviled Middle Ages. For instance, the powerful cardinal Raffaele Riario, nephew of Pope Sixtus IV, demolished the church of San Lorenzo in Damaso to build his Palazzo della Cancelleria, and placed the Augustan-era Roman columns from the church's nave in his courtyard. The palace's *Sala dei cento giorni* (the 'Hall of a hundred days', for the time it took the artist to paint it) was later adorned by Giorgio Vasari with a series of frescoes in honour of Paul III, which include portraits of several of Pietro's friends, such as Reginald Pole and Jacopo Sadoleto, and probably also a likeness of Pietro.

During the second decade of the sixteenth century, Rome gained not only many beautiful new palaces and suburban villas, designed and built by artists such as Donato Bramante, Raphael, or Antonio and Giuliano da Sangallo, but also a new street plan, consisting of long straight avenues linking the city's various centres of power. The Via Alessandrina extended from the Vatican to Castel Sant'Angelo; the kilometre-long Via Giulia ran from Ponte Sisto to san Giovanni dei Fiorentini; and the Via della Lungara skirted the banks of the Tiber, past Agostino Chigi's villa. The latter two were drawn by the architect Donato Bramante, who also designed the new Basilica of St Peter and several famous palaces. Meanwhile, Michelangelo finished the ceiling of the Sistine Chapel and Raphael decorated the apartments of Julius II in the Vatican with some of his most famous works, including the *School of Athens* in the Stanza della Segnatura. Michelangelo, for his part, seemed poised to revive the glory of classical sculpture with his *Bacchus* [Figure 25], created for Cardinal Riario, and his *Pietà*, commissioned by Cardinal Jean de Bilhères-Lagraulas and probably completed before July 1500, which now stands in the Vatican.

Such was the electrifying atmosphere that greeted Pietro on his arrival in Rome. The arts were flourishing with unprecedented splendour, and the popes, in their largesse, bankrolled an endless stream of magnificent entertainments and festivities suitable for every taste and interest. And Pietro's tastes were chiefly cultural. In Rome as in Urbino, he surrounded himself with a group of friends with whom he explored the city and its surroundings. In a famous letter to Bibbiena dated 3 April 1516, he describes a projected expedition to Tivoli:

> Tomorrow, Navagero, Beazzano, Messer Baldassarre Castiglione, Raphael and I plan to go to Tivoli, which I last visited twenty-seven years ago. We shall discover what is old and what is new, and see all that is beautiful in the area. We are going as a favour to M. Andrea, who will leave for Venice after the day of Pasquino.

Andrea Navagero was a Humanist and historian of the Republic; Beazzano was Agostino Bevazzano, a poet and Humanist like Pietro. The two men appear in a double portrait painted in 1516 by Raphael, which once belonged to Pietro [Figure 26].

From behind that aristocratic screen, on which figures of remarkable humanists can be observed wandering through the ruins of Tivoli and studying the remains of Antiquity, the raucous, ribald revelry of Pasquino emerges. It was probably at some time in that same year that a young poet arrived in Rome from Perugia, and became the mask and alter ego of Pasquino. He was Pietro Aretino, 'il divino Pietro', the scourge of princes.

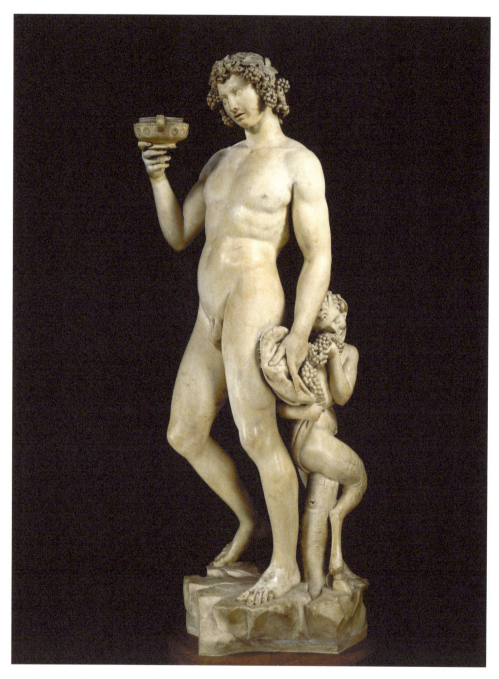

Fig. 25. Michelangelo, *Bacchus*, 1497, marble, height 203 cm, Museo Nazionale del Bargello, Florence. © 2015. Photo Scala, Florence; courtesy of the Ministero Beni e Att. Culturali

Fig. 26. Raphael, *Double portrait (Andrea Navagero and Agostino Bevazzano)*, c. 1516, oil on canvas, 76 × 107 cm, Doria Pamphilj Gallery, Rome. Amministrazione Doria Pamphilj srl con socio unico

The function of the double portrait was to immortalise this group of friends before they parted ways. Under Pietro's watchful gaze, the two friends would remain forever as Raphael's paintbrush had caught them, engrossed in conversation. But the portrait would inevitably remind him of the fourth friend, the young prodigy who died on 6 April 1520, four years after his letter to Bibbiena.

There is another valuable document recounting Pietro's life in Rome. It is a letter he sent to Bernardo Dovizi da Bibbiena, on 19 April of the same year 1516, in which he describes a portrait by Raphael of Antonio Tebaldeo, a friend from Ferrara, compared to which his portraits of Baldassarre Castiglione or Guidubaldo da Montefeltro were like the work of apprentices. He freely admitted that he was jealous — he often coveted works in the collections of his friends and acquaintances, and not infrequently tried to acquire them, by means that were sometimes less than courteous. He wonderfully sums up the essence of the portrait and of Raphael's artistry at its apogee: 'He painted our Tebaldeo so well that the same Tebaldeo resembles himself less than this portrait does'. That brilliant formulation is reminiscent of Raphael's epitaph, traditionally ascribed to Pietro, visible to this day above the painter's tomb in the Pantheon: 'Ille hic est Raphael, timuit quo sospite vinci | rerum magna parens et moriente mori', 'Here lies Raphael by whom Nature feared to be conquered while he lived and, when he was dying, feared herself to die.' The rest of the letter transports the reader to Pietro's study, almost as if one were looking over his shoulder as he wrote:

> As I sit writing this letter, Raphael has just arrived, as if he had guessed that I was speaking of him. He asks me to add the following message: could you please send him more stories for your *stufetta*, because this week he expects to finish painting the ones you gave him last time. My goodness, I can hardly believe it, M. Baldassar has just arrived too [...].

The friends whose memory was to be preserved in their absence by their portraits, appear, as if by magic, in the reality of the letter, which in passing provides some information about another remarkable project, the frescoes in Cardinal Bibbiena's *stufetta* in the Vatican. Raphael decorated the *stufetta*, a type of small bathroom also used as a sort of sauna or steam bath, with scenes from the myth of Venus and Cupid, as well as marbles, statues, niches, figures of animals and *putti*. The lunettes were decorated with *grottesche* on a ground of Pompeian red. Raphael's work evoked both a Roman interior and the room's function as a place of pleasure, the stimulation of which was no doubt the chief purpose of the mythical decorative scheme, for these heated rooms were often used during the Renaissance for pursuits of a more frankly erotic nature.

In Book III, Chapter I of his masterpiece *Prose della volgar lingua*, Bembo painted a portrait of Rome that is both concise and, in its way, perfect. The city he depicted was burdened with memories of its ancient past and teeming with artists eager to emulate both nature and classical models. The 'infinite relics' scattered everywhere by time and the enemy attracted artists in droves. They studied the ancient marble or copper statues displayed in public places or private collections, sketched them onto paper, or reproduced them in wax models. But there were also arches, baths, theatres and many other ancient buildings; the artists attempted to reproduce them, judging the merits of their realisations according to how closely they emulated their sublime models, which had attained a degree of perfection unsurpassed by any other work of art. Raphael and Michelangelo eclipsed all their peers in this respect, and could justifiably be compared to the great masters of antiquity. Yet none of this would have existed without writing. No one would have heard of Myron, Phidias, Apelles, Vitruvius or Leon Battista Alberti — a great Humanist and outstanding architect, painter and writer — had they not been celebrated first in writing. Pietro thus took an active part in a tradition that his friends had carried to perfection, and positioned himself, in a manner of speaking, at its apex.

The *Prose* implicitly foreshadowed the events that would unfold two years later, since what had befallen ancient Rome could also happen to modern Rome. Only writing could ensure that those wonderful achievements would survive forever. Although published only in 1525, after Pietro had left Rome — he returned in 1524 to present the dedicatory manuscript to Pope Clement VII — the *Prose* would have been unimaginable without that background. In his masterpiece, Pietro urged writers to follow the example of great creators and artists and assiduously study the classics in order to perfect the art of writing, especially in the vernacular, since Latin had already been thoroughly explored. By that time, the classics included the great authors of the fourteenth century — Dante, Petrarch and Boccaccio — and the Provençal writers who invented the romance form. Pietro was one of the first to systematically study that genre, thanks in part to the ready availability in Venice of some of the oldest and most representative manuscripts of Provençal lyric poetry, many of which could be found in the private libraries of his close acquaintances. In 1530, he mentioned in a letter to his friend Tebaldeo that he planned to publish several of these romances with biographies of their authors.

Pietro's time in Rome, though highly significant, was relatively uneventful. He revised his poems, worked on the *Prose* and wrote papal briefs. He received his first ecclesiastical benefits, but also suffered several professional setbacks. More specifically, his ties to Venice, already weakened by the events of the past decade, grew increasingly strained. In December 1514, the pope sent him on an embassy to his native city with the task of persuading the Republic to join him in a league against the French. But the doge Leonardo Loredan had no intention of complying with the request of the pope and his ambassador, as Pietro informed his superiors in several long, contrite letters. He nonetheless penned a long missive to the doge, explaining that, as a good citizen of Venice, he believed it was in the Republic's best interest to meet the pope's demands, because, as he proudly declared:

> Believing myself, by my Venetian birth, to have been born in the greatest city and nation of the world, I cannot ignore the great love and tenderness I feel towards her. Moreover, I have never had any inclination or desire to learn the art of deceit and flattery, which is why I decided to live far from my homeland, for without that talent it is difficult to find one's place here. So, I believe, and you will certainly agree with me, that, in this respect, I have not shirked my duty.

With its strange mix of insistence, accusation, patriotism and pride, this letter amply demonstrates that the old wound of his break with Venice still festered.

Pietro's old and new wounds, setbacks and disappointments were exacerbated by the death of many old friends around the same time: il Magnifico Giuliano in 1516, Bibbiena and Raphael in 1520. But without a doubt the most painful loss was that of his father, on 28 May 1519. Shortly before his death, Pietro asked for leave of absence to convalesce from a grave illness he had contracted in the early months of 1518. On 1 August 1518, he wrote to Bibbiena informing him that he had slowly recovered over the previous twenty days, and was beginning to 'overcome [...] this anxiety, lack of natural vigour, and low fever'. He shaved for the first time in months and, though still unsteady, ventured out for short strolls among the cedars, laurels and myrtles of Rome, especially during the cooler hours of the day. In April of the following year, Pietro left the papal city in the hope of making a complete recovery. He received the news of his father's death in Bologna, but could not reach Venice until after the funeral.

He stayed in his native city until March 1520, in part to organise the marriage of his niece Marcella to Giovan Matteo Bembo, a nephew. Giovan Matteo went on to make a brilliant career as a commander of the Venetian fleet, a politician and eventually a member of the Council of Ten, like Bernardo but unlike Pietro. A cultivated man who counted many writers among his friends, Giovan Matteo corresponded frequently with his uncle; their letters were collected and published in 1564. Pietro described these events to Bibbiena in a long and beautiful answer to a letter of condolence from the cardinal, which brings to light Pietro's contradictory emotions (the letter is dated 1 October 1519). He mentions the 'bitterness and melancholy in his soul' following the loss of his father, but then seems eager to move on to other topics: 'regarding the words of consolation you offered for the grief caused by the loss of my good and sainted father [...] I have already resolved to accept it, as you instructed me to'. The letter details his various health problems — kidney pains, catarrh — and describes his walks, outings on horseback, and the delight he feels when breathing the air of home. Yet his soul was still troubled, not so much by his father's death as by the fact that it 'has left me with so many obligations that I don't know which way to turn'. Although he wanted to 'defend my pleasant little house' — his property in Noniano — the manager of his *benefici* in Bologna had stolen over six hundred gold florins from him over the past year. Not only were his medical costs escalating, but 'In addition to all those tribulations, I have had to see to the marriage of my niece and give her a dowry of three thousand florins [...], not in money but in the form of income which formerly came to me and will now go to her husband, as well as a few hundred florins in cash'. He had plenty more to worry about: there were also 'two other grown nieces, both of marriageable age, who depend on me'. Then, finally, a ray of sunshine: 'But enough about those worries! I gave my oldest niece, Marcella, to a worthy and virtuous man, M. Giovan Mateo Bembo, who is both a relative and a compatriot. Though not wealthy, he is comfortably well-off, and highly esteemed and respected in this city, considering that he is only twenty-eight'.

In this involuntarily colourful self-portrait, the author appears under the guise of the tight-fisted old codger in a farce, who is forced to take a wife or marry off his son, and is forever counting the bags of florins he has piled up over a lifetime of saving — not unlike the character of Messer Nicias in a mordant comedy by a Florentine author, probably from 1518, which was popular around that time, and was performed in Venice, in 1522, around carnival. The play, *Mandragola*, was by a certain Niccolò Machiavelli. Despite his ill-tempered complaining and moaning, and though always acutely attentive to his personal welfare — his florins, medicines and ailments — Pietro could at times be generous. Marcella's wedding was expensive but worthy of the Bembos, and his heart rejoiced when he wrote about Giovan Matteo. Moreover, he let it be known that when the time came for his two other nieces to wed they would receive a handsome dowry, perhaps from an ecclesiastical benefice.

In April 1520, Pietro returned to Rome. However, he soon realised that, due in part to his health and in part to a noticeable change in the political climate, there was little room for him there. The following spring, he went back to Padua and then on to Venice, where he stayed until February 1522, before establishing his permanent residence in Padua. Pope Leo X was dead, and the magnificent Rome of Pietro's memories had disappeared with him. He was succeeded by Adrian VI, a Dutchman from Utrecht who had been Charles V's tutor. The new pope was a stranger to Rome, and the Romans, accustomed to the opulence of Leo X, balked at his rigorous style. Moreover, he was a tutor, or 'pedant', a term that at the time was inevitably taken to imply that he was also a sodomite. After he died, Pietro Aretino, hiding behind the mask of Pasquino, exulted in a fierce poem:

> Even in the last years of his life,
> he was a mean, doddering old fool,
> infatuated with young men.
> In the end, he died in his palace
> like an animal [...].

Adrian IV ordered Pietro to take his ecclesiastical vows, as for several years he had been the recipient of substantial ecclesiastical benefices without being ordained. In December 1522, he therefore took vows, including one of chastity. In November 1523, a son, Lucilio, was born. Another son, Torquato, came into the world on 10 May 1525, followed by a daughter, Elena, on 30 June 1528. Their mother, Morosina, was probably Pietro's last great love. She was born Ambrogina Faustina, the daughter of Antonio Della Torre, from Genoa. She met Pietro in 1513 and was his companion until her death, on 6 August 1535. The relationship was certainly less passionate than Pietro's love for Maria or Lucrezia, but much steadier. Morosina may have been married; indeed, her sister Mariola's will implies that her husband was alive in 1525, but does not name him. Pietro met Morosina when she was around sixteen, but it seems that he first saw her when she was eight: in a letter to his friend Cosimo Gheri, dated February 1537, he remarked that his daughter Elena was growing more graceful by the day and would certainly become a very beautiful woman, since her mother Morosina was not nearly as pretty at her age. Cosimo, he added, must remember how charming Morosina had been, though he had met her when she was no longer in the flower of youth ('iam deflorescente'), shortly before her death at the age of thirty-eight. The letter thus indicates that Morosina was born in 1497, making her twenty-seven years younger than Pietro. Thanks to the sonnets, we also know her age at death and the duration of her relationship with Pietro: exactly twenty-two years.

Pietro, now in his fifties, was experiencing a second youth, like a long and golden Indian summer. Finally unshackled from the vicissitudes of court life, he was free to divide his time between Padua and Venice; he had become a father; Morosina and his friend Cola Bruno were always by his side. Having recovered his health and energy, he completed his greatest masterpiece, the *Prose della volgar lingua*. Renaissance artists often represented Fortune as bald except for a single lock of hair in front to symbolise how difficult she was to catch. Pietro, as we have seen, knew a thing or two about women's hair, and his hands, despite the injury inflicted many years ago by Giusto Goro, where still strong enough to seize passing Fortune's forelock. Adrian VI reigned for only a few years. In November 1523, his successor was chosen: Clement VII, another Medici pope. This new development revived Pietro's professional ambitions, which he had never completely abandoned. About a year later, in October 1524, after finishing the *Prose*, he left for Rome to serve the new pontiff.

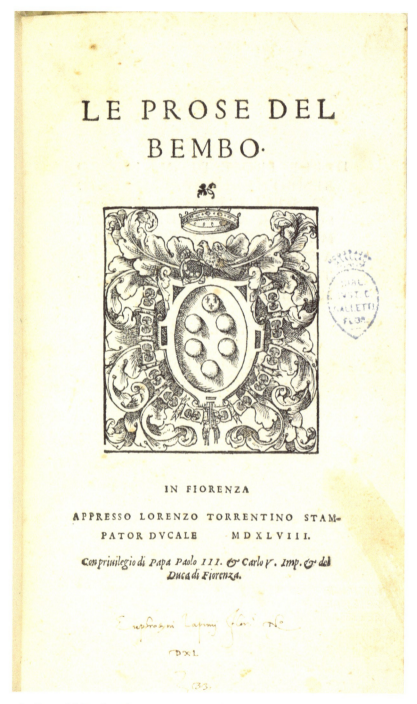

FIG. 27. *Le Prose del Bembo,* Florence, Lorenzo Torrentino, Stampatore ducale, 1548, title page. Fondation Barbier-Mueller pour l'étude de la poésie italienne de la Renaissance, University of Geneva. Fondation Barbier-Mueller pour l'étude de la poésie italienne de la Renaissance, University of Geneva

CHAPTER 8

The Common Father of Letters

The 10th of December 1503 was a cold and windy day. A freezing north wind buffeted the lagoon, as three gentlemen hurried through the streets of Venice, pressed against the walls. They were going to the house of a common friend, for a celebratory birthday luncheon. When they finally arrived at Carlo Bembo's house, Federico Fregoso, Il Magnifico Giuliano de' Medici and the aged and infirm Ercole Strozzi were relieved to discover a blaze roaring in the great fireplace. After the meal, Ercole drew his chair closer to the fire. One imagines him holding out his palms to the crackling flames. All of a sudden, a seemingly futile discussion arose among the group of friends. Il Magnifico Giuliano complained of the *rovaio* seeping through the cracks in the leaded glass of the windows. What did he mean, they asked him? *Rovaio* was the name given by the Florentines to the cold north wind, Giuliano explained. But the word was unknown in Venice, Ferrara and Genoa, where his companions came from. And so, in the course of a discussion about the language spoken in Florence, the four friends laid the foundations of Italian as it would be spoken for centuries afterwards. Or so Bembo would have us believe, in his account in *Prose della volgar lingua* [Figure 27].

The *Prose*, published in 1525, was repeatedly revised and corrected until the last moment. But in his narrative, Bembo depicts it as the result of that long-distant discussion, and claims to have written most of the book before 1515. The truth of the matter is that by the mid-1520s Bembo needed to consolidate his reputation. He planned to do so by providing the Italian people with a grammar and style guide, which, thanks to the many examples it contained, could also serve as a history of classical Italian literature. As we have seen, the great authors of the fourteenth century provided the foundation for this project, which he had been mulling over for many years and had already partly put into practice. But someone beat him to it: in 1516, a scholar from Friuli-Venezia Giulia, Giovan Francesco Fortunio, published an Italian grammar entitled *Regole grammaticali della volgar lingua*. He died the following year, and therefore no longer posed a threat to Bembo. But the latter could tolerate no challenge to his supremacy and hence antedated his grammar, somewhat disingenuously, to a year before Fortunio's. In 1529, in a letter to Bernardo Tasso, Torquato's father, he came close to accusing the late grammarian of stealing his ideas. Actually, if anyone profited from the work of another, it was unquestionably Pietro, since Fortunio first applied for permission to publish a grammar book in 1509.

What is certain is that, in the first decade of the sixteenth century, the need for a common language that could be universally recognised as *Italian* was felt strongly in Venice. Yet in 1525, to impose his model, Pietro still found it necessary to discredit all previous works that could potentially overshadow his. He was in fact playing a double game: he hoped to permanently establish his authority in the world of letters with this new book, while simultaneously regaining his influence with the Italian courts.

Pietro immediately understood that two steps were necessary to achieve his goal. He obtained first the strategic support of the pope, to whom the *Prose* were dedicated, and then that of Giovan Matteo Giberti, the powerful *datario* (the papal official responsible for distributing ecclesiastic benefices), who became Bishop of Verona in August 1524. To Giberti, he dedicated a Latin poem on a mythological theme, entitled *Benacus*, the Latin name of Lake Garda. The poem recounts how Benacus, hearing about the young man who has come to govern Verona, invites all the neighbouring rivers — the Lambro, Ticino, Adda and Po — to a banquet generously watered with Cretan wine. Underneath the crystalline surface of the aquatic fantasy lurked the memory of the recent wars, and the ghostly presence of the cities and fields of the Venetian countryside abandoned by their inhabitants and deserted by their peasants. The poem praises the exceptional qualities of a young man dearly loved by the pope and the gods. France, Spain, the Adriatic Sea and lastly Rome are summoned as witnesses (Giovan Matteo Giberti travelled widely as the pope's ambassador). In Bembo's imagination, all of Nature prepared to pay homage to the young man who had recently arrived in the land of Venice: tender grass blanketed the earth, leaves covered the trees, the vines were laden with grapes, and the rivers and lakes teemed with fish. Nymphs presented him with baskets overflowing with marjoram, lilies and hyacinths. After many years of war, a new age of peace covered the martyred land with flowers, colours and scent, just as the rains after a torrid summer bring nature back to life. But the courtly tribute and limpid verse could not obscure the troubling presence of war, as if, for Pietro, some form of turbulence must always undermine the idyll that he ostensibly searched for his entire life. The poem once more demonstrates Pietro's mythological and antiquarian tastes, as well as a sensual vein already visible in other poems. The personification of the water gods appears again in the Latin poem *Sarc*, a declaration of love to Lake Garda and Venice, which recounts the birth of Lake Garda as the result of the River Sarca's passion for his small-breasted daughter Garda, with a refined sensuality vaguely reminiscent of Raphael's aesthetic.

For Pietro, several essentially peaceful years lay ahead. The preceding decades had seen him in perpetual movement, preoccupied with the task of defining a cultural identity while securing his position on the Italian stage. Now, finally, he could devote himself entirely to managing and consolidating his achievements. Of course, the affairs of his household and his many ecclesiastical benefices sometimes brought him headaches. And there were deaths to mourn, and sorrows to bear. Literary disputes, too, which could turn brutal, sometimes with surprisingly tragic results. Still, Pietro seems to have enjoyed a period of several years after the publication of the *Prose* during which he was able to devote himself fully to reviewing, improving and perfecting his writing. He had a clear objective in mind: to build his literary monument. To do so, he needed to provide his readers with reliable, up-to-date and easily available editions of everything he had ever written. His first priority was therefore to devise a careful editorial plan and find a printer equal to the task. In 1530, he decided to entrust the publication of his collected works to Giovanni Antonio Nicolini da Sabbio and his brothers, a family of typographers and printers from the area of Brescia. The Nicolini brothers apprenticed under Andrea Torresani, Aldo Manuzio's father-in-law; in a sense, Pietro had come full circle. Andrea Torresani's workshop came to a standstill after his death in 1528, as the Manuzio and Torresani families battled over the inheritance. Neither social nor family ties carried much weight with Aldo Manuzio's ambitious young son Paolo, who was determined to restore the past glory of his father's workshop and assert his rights. The row ended in a stalemate. By contrast, the Nicolini brothers were newcomers to the Venetian printing industry, having made their debut in 1522 with a book on the abundance and diversity of the Latin tongue, by Niccolò Liburnio, a grammarian who also authored several other grammatical treatises (*Le tre fontane*, *Le vulgari eleganzie*) that directly rivalled the *Prose* (*Le tre fontane* was printed in 1526). In 1530, Pietro entrusted the publication of his *Rime* and a revised second edition of *Gli Asolani* to the Nicolini press. He also brought out second editions of *De Ætna* and *De Urbini ducibus*, simultaneously with *De imitatione* and *De Virgilii Culice*. In this way, Bembo, by then in his sixties, hoped to bring his work to the attention of a new generation of authors writing in Italian, whom he imagined congregating in spirit — or sometimes in the flesh, as his guests in Noniano — around him, their unchallenged master.

In reality, there were many polemics. Some readers met Bembo's position with indifference; others deliberately distanced themselves (such as his friend Castiglione, who, in the *Cortegiano*, took a very different approach, opting to write in the language most familiar to him as a native of Mantua rather than attempting to express himself in fourteenth-century Tuscan). Others yet, more unexpectedly, openly mocked him. The poet and promising young scholar Antonio Brocardo, for instance, in the course of a discussion with his peers, ridiculed the rules laid down by the 'dictator of letters', but he died suddenly a year later, in 1531. Pietro Aretino rejoiced, and went so far as to take credit for his untimely demise, claiming that his sonnets, which mocked Brocardo's Jewish origins, caused the latter to die of a broken heart. The Brocardo episode is full of shadows and contradictions; all its protagonists appear simultaneously indifferent to his tragic demise and surprised, even moved, by its suddenness. The affair did not reflect well on Bembo. For many years, Aretino boasted with cruel arrogance that he was the author of the 'sonnet that killed Brocardo' (letter to Francesco dell'Arme, 15 May 1537). Many years later, in 1553, in a letter to Giovanni Giustinian di Candia, he again mocked him cruelly: 'Ha, ha, ha! Do you want to know what makes me laugh? Those stupid fools who believe the rumour that the sonnets against Brocardo are not by me but by Messer Cola of Bembo. [...] The late Antonio would still be alive today if that man, who never thought of writing them, had indeed composed them in Padua! For they would have turned for him into bread and grapes to eat rather than poison and absinth'. However, around the same time, in December 1537, he sent four laudatory sonnets in memory of Brocardo to Brevio in a letter in which he expressed regret for 'the death he brought upon himself by offending the divine Bembo, whose name is worshipped in the Temple of Eternity'. And Bembo? In a letter dated 21 August 1531, Brevio wrote to Aretino that Pietro was 'infinitely sorry'. By contrast, several years later, Benedetto Varchi, a Florentine living in Padua (the author of Bembo's funeral oration), paints a more disquieting picture in a letter to Aretino, in October 1536: 'Monsignor Bembo, with whom I spoke of you yesterday on the boat, praised you fulsomely and seems to hold you in great affection. He told me about the time when you caused Brocardo's death and a thousand other things'. The flippant tone of this anecdote, in the context of a boat excursion on the Brenta River, seems to jar with the tragic nature of the event it refers to, which ought to have saddened the future cardinal. At any rate, his most diligent defender — the other Pietro — attacked other critics too, including a certain Ubaldino Baldinelli who censured a collection of *brevi* written by Bembo on behalf of Leo X, which the former published in 1535. In a sonnet, Aretino excoriated Baldinelli while flattering Pietro:

> A Florentine plebeian named Ubaldino
> destroys and criticises Bembo's *brevi*
> to show off his superior culture to his master.
> A man of the pen, a lover of women and wine,
> good Pietro is deaf to his barking,
> for the lion doesn't fight the hare,
> nor the eagle attack the sparrow.

It is unclear whether the 'eagle of Noniano' was hiding behind the polemic and its fatal outcome (if the traditional account is true) or simply stood by and let others do as they pleased. What is certain is that Bembo was careful never to jeopardise his good relations with Pietro Aretino.

In fact, controversies like the one described above were not uncommon. A touchy lot at the best of times, the humanists were particularly unnerved by the unbridled capitalistic tendencies of the printing industry. Theft, plagiarism and pirate editions were economically ruinous, while literary rows, such as the one that overwhelmed Giovan Francesco Fortunio, could destroy one's reputation. A man as careful as Bembo when it came to his revenues and his interests could not afford to compromise, and indeed showed himself unyielding in defending them. Between 1527 and 1528, for instance, he broke off all relations with Giberti, to whom he had dedicated *Benacus* three years earlier, and with the Pio family, with whom he had been connected since a young age. The *casus belli* was the abbey of Badia di Rosazzo, near Udine, which Giberti had promised to Pietro, only to give it to Rodolfo Pio, much to the former's disappointment, since it brought in twelve hundred florins a year. Blinded by greed, Pietro fought long and hard for what he saw as his due, although the abbey itself was not particularly attractive. A mordant description of the Badia appears in a 1528 sonnet by Giberti's secretary, the famous Florentine scholar Francesco Berni, the *Sonetto in descrizione di una Badia*. The first verses are brutally lapidary: 'My Lord, I have discovered an abbey that looks like the goddess of destruction'. The quarrel no doubt affected Pietro deeply, yet his self-regard emerged unscathed: 'if you do not give me the abbey that I rightly deserve, I shall nevertheless remain Pietro Bembo,' he wrote to Giberti on 31 August 1527. And in case the prelate still did not understand, he repeated the point on 28 January of the following year: 'the men who come after us [...] will decide who, of M. Giovan Matteo Ghiberto or M. Pietro Bembo, in all the years and days of his life, attained the highest positions and revenues, the best studies and most admired works.'

An extraordinary event the following year rekindled Bembo's pride and compensated somewhat for his recent frustrations: the coronation of Charles V in Bologna. On the same occasion, a universal peace was to be signed between France and the Empire, and the Church and the Empire. After years of war and the destruction of Rome, the great powers had finally come to an agreement, bringing a welcome respite to an exhausted Italy. On 5 November, Charles V arrived in Bologna. The peace was signed on 23 December and publicly announced on the 31st. On 24 February, Charles V was crowned by the pope, and a great celebration followed. Seven thousand men arrived in Bologna in the impressive imperial entourage, along with the flower of the Italian nobility and all the greatest writers and scholars of the time.

The coronation was also a significant event from a literary — even linguistic — perspective. Romolo Quirino Amaseo, a professor of Latin and Greek at the University of Bologna, gave an oration in Latin entitled *De pace* (On Peace), followed by a further two speeches, *De latinæ linguæ usu retinendo* (On the Use and Preservation of Latin). In both, he argued that the use of Latin was necessary in a university city as ancient as Bologna, and, more importantly, that Latin possessed an inherent dignity and capacity to connect with the great institutions of the past. The coronation was a celebration of imperial continuity, since Charles V, although he received his crown from the hands of Pope Clement VII, was already the undisputed master of Europe. This implied a shift in the cultural centre of gravity from Italy to Imperial Europe, that is, Spain and Germany. A new Humanism, founded and disseminated by the school of Erasmus of Rotterdam, was already flourishing on the other side of the Alps. To assert the primacy of Latin, therefore, was a step backward, which robbed Italy of its last shred of independence. In a bold and astute move, the Italian scholars, led by Bembo and Castiglione, chose exactly that moment to propose their own models. The popularity of Castiglione's *Cortegiano* and Bembo's Petrarchan style all across Europe was not fortuitous: it was the only way to avoid complete marginalisation.

That context in large part explains why Bembo published a second edition of his *oeuvre* in 1530, a year that marked a decisive turning point for Europe, and especially Italy. The final curtain had fallen on the world of the Italian courts of the fifteenth and early sixteenth centuries, the stage on which Pietro had played a starring role. To maintain a certain margin of manoeuvre in that new political environment, characterised by the dominance of a small number of national or supranational states rather than a plethora of small courts, intellectuals needed to address the many challenges of the age and come up with new models, starting with language — or risk slow extinction in a sad and obscure menagerie, disconnected from the outside world. And that is exactly what they did over the next few decades.

A critical game was afoot in Bologna. But it was also a time of levity and celebration, parties, banquets, jousts and discussions among the authors invited to take part in the festivities. The magnificence of the imperial procession is described by Isabella d'Este in a letter to Renée of France. First came three cavalry companies armed with lances, followed by the artillery, sappers and fourteen companies of infantry. Next came the cavalry of Burgundy in green, yellow and red uniforms, accompanied by armed pages and followed by the king's gentlemen, with pages decked out in multicoloured jackets and yellow velvet caps. The emperor was preceded by a man holding a sword and wearing a tabard of gold brocade, which laid bare his chest and right arm. Then came the gentlemen of Bologna, in white satin with pink stockings and feathered hats. During the parade, gold and silver coins were tossed to the crowd. A few dramatic episodes threw a pall over the festivities, however; the most infamous was the massacre of eighteen Spanish cavalrymen on the night of 21 March. Isabella's entourage included a number of young women who took advantage of the festive atmosphere, heightened by the proximity of carnival, to indulge in rather free and licentious behaviour. The jousts, masques and parties organised daily often continued all night long. Jealous rivalries soon broke out between the Spaniards and local youths. Insults and obscene drawings were scrawled in chalk and charcoal on the walls of the palace where Isabella was staying. The quarrel finally degenerated into a massacre. The scandal forced Isabella to leave with her retinue of unruly young ladies. All this must have been like a great carnival play, complete with banquets, orgies, balls and donations of money. Deep down, though, the image of the emperor kneeling to kiss the pope's slipper was a form of theatre, for the foot he kissed belonged to the same Medici pope who had witnessed the unprecedented pillages, rapes and terrible exactions visited upon the holy city and its inhabitants by the imperial troops while he was imprisoned in Castel Sant'Angelo.

Francesco Berni clearly understood the absurdity of the situation; it inspired his satirical poem, *L'entrata dell'imperadore in Bologna*. The first part of the poem, in the manner of a nursery rhyme, lists a series of easily identifiable characters with funny names, paired with invented names signifying their opposite, as if to ridicule the solemn, triumphant appearance of the imperial procession: 'Battista Cazzetto [small cock] — Antonio della Coscia [thigh]; Vincenzio Gambacorta [short leg] — Vergilio Gambalunga [long leg]; Francesco Calcagno [heel] — Andrea dell'Unghia [fingernail]', and so on. The list is followed by a satirical account of the progress of the imperial parade through various parts of the city, which is full of obscene and utterly untranslatable puns involving food items and sexual organs: 'Sguazza Coie [...] di poi passò per Paglia in culo, per il Borgo delle ballotte, per l'Inferno, per Gierusalem, Quartirolo, Gatta marcia, Pizza morti [...] Fiacca 'l collo, Truffa il mondo, Frega Tette [...]. E sua maiestà se n'andò in San Petronio e dipoi in palazzo. Dove fu poi da' bolognesi presentato di cuccole, salsizuotti, calcini, leccaboni.' With this riotous procession of phallic sausages and other suggestive delicacies, a crucial period in the cultural and political life of the sixteenth century was drawing to a close. Between the lines of Berni's poem one glimpses a new awareness that the Italian Renaissance was now well and truly dead and buried.

This period of intense activity and difficult choices was marked by many deaths. In 1529, two of Bembo's oldest friends died: Baldassarre Castiglione in February and Andrea Navagero in May. Both were living abroad at the time, in France and Spain respectively. Pietro did not obtain permission to visit them one last time. During the same few months, Luigi da Porto succumbed to a malignant fever, as did Girolamo Savorgnan. 'Accursed be these days of ill fortune!' Pietro exclaimed, ruing fate for depriving him of so many dear friends. But worse was still to come. Two years later, in the stifling heat of August, his beloved son Lucilio died in Padua. Pietro, by then past sixty-five, had only Elena and Torquato left, and of course the faithful and affectionate Cola Bruno.

But more storm clouds were gathering in the sky over Noniano. The death of Pietro's brother Bartolomeo in 1526 brought new worries. The latter's son Carlo was not unlike the *pazzerone* Giusto Goro whom Pietro fought in his youth. If anything, Carlo was wilder. On a stifling day in summer, Pietro was lying in bed, racked by a violent fever. In the room next to his, three jugs had been set on the windowsill; the first contained boiled water, the second barley water and the third an infusion of medicinal herbs. From his sick bed, Pietro asked for a bowl of soup and a glass of wine cut with a little boiled water. After eating and drinking, Pietro felt a sudden burning sensation in his throat. His servant Giovanni Antonio, who ate with him, experienced the same symptoms. Cola Bruno immediately understood what had happened; on inspecting the jugs, he noticed that they had changed colour, and there were traces of a deadly poison made from mercury on the spouts. The doctors were summoned at once. They directed Pietro and his servant to drink a cupful of oil to induce vomiting, but the treatment did not work for Pietro. The doctors then administered a purgative tablet called a *bolo armeno*. Pietro finally regurgitated the contents of his stomach into a cup, which immediately turned black. The mysterious poisoner was unlucky, for if Pietro had drunk from the two other jugs as well, he would most certainly have died. The *podestà* of Padua put a price on the assassin's head: a thousand ducats alive, eight hundred dead. The authorities opened an investigation. Their suspicions soon converged on Carlo, although he was in Rome at the time, possibly sent there by Pietro in the hope that the papal city would encourage him to change his ways. Pietro survived this new ordeal and was well enough by October to joke about it with Soranzo. The nephew whom he had favoured with the income from his Badia di Villanova, he wrote, 'seeing that the fever was not treating me well enough to his taste, gave me poison,' which was no surprise since he was an 'evil, cruel boy who may well have poisoned others before me'. Banned from Venice, he disappeared and was soon forgotten.

The year was 1530. Pietro had survived the fever and the poisoning, and was preparing to publish his collected works. As if this was not enough to exhaust a man who was no longer in the flower of youth, he was named librarian and historian of the Republic of Venice. He delegated the former responsibility in part to his friends Ramusio, Giovan Matteo Bembo and Benedetto Ramberti, to whom he finally bequeathed the position in 1543. The second position involved the exhausting task of recording, in elegant Latin prose, the event of the past few decades of Venice's convulsive political history. Ironically, it fell to a man he needed to complete this task for whom Venetian politics had chiefly been a source of bitter disappointment.

Pietro thought he had found just the man in the person of the noble — but old, ill and impoverished — chronicler Marino Sanudo. For years, Sanudo had wandered the city daily in search of news, sat on the Council, questioned noblemen, copied letters, read dispatches and analysed ambassadors' reports. He wrote constantly, filling dozens of volumes with his cramped hand. He also copied vernacular translations of the comedies of Plautus, poems and pamphlets in manuscripts, which he proudly inscribed 'Est Marini Sanuti Leonardi filii' (Belonging to Marino Sanudo, son of Leonardo). For many years, Marino dreamed of becoming the historiographer of the Republic, but all his attempts were unsuccessful. Navagero, the official historian, burned all his papers shortly before he died, leaving no trace of the work he claimed to have been writing, and Sanudo doubted that he had ever written a single page. In the eyes of this stern and gruff servant of the Republic, Bembo's friend had pocketed the official historian's handsome fee without doing a stroke of work, whereas Sanudo had sacrificed everything to the Fatherland, acting as its actual historiographer for several decades, in the privacy of his study, without receiving a single ducat for his pains. But his dream of succeeding Navagero was disappointed. His rival had the immense advantage of a famous name. And not content with resorting to what must have seemed to Sanudo like a theft, Pietro, although he had abandoned Venice a quarter century earlier — a reprehensible act in itself — had the audacity to knock on his door in San Giacomo dell'Orio, asking to borrow his precious manuscripts so that he might exploit the wealth of information they contained. What impudence! Sanudo proudly refused.

In the end, Pietro had the greatest difficulty obtaining the manuscript and asked Doge Andrea Gritti to intercede. At first he complained to him directly: in a letter of August 1531, he said that he had seen Sanudo's 'histories' that past winter and mentioned, somewhat dismissively, that they contained 'many things of little importance' which might nonetheless help him complete the mission entrusted to him by the Signoria. And what was the old historian's response? That 'these books represented the work and efforts of an entire life, and that he had no desire to make a gift of his sweat to anyone.' How unbelievably impertinent! If Gritti could not force the stubborn Marino to comply, Pietro would address himself directly to the heads of the Council of Ten. Which is exactly what he did in September; since the doge was too busy to comply with his request, he wrote, the Council must persuade Sanudo to lend him the manuscripts, as it was in the interest of their Lordships and the Fatherland. And so Pietro, in his sixties, threw himself into this difficult, obstacle-strewn endeavour.

Reaching the age of sixty in that day and age put a heavy burden on a man. But Pietro had energy to spare. It happened to be a time in which several old men blessed with an extraordinary vitality profoundly influenced the course of history and culture. Two of those men, whom Pietro later met, lived in Rome, and one of them was to play a decisive role in his final years. They were Alessandro Farnese, who became Pope Paul III in 1534, and Michelangelo Buonarroti. The new pope was two years older than Pietro; Michelangelo was five years younger. Their education, which they completed before the end of the fifteenth century, widened the divide between them and the new generation born around 1500. Like them, Pietro seemed to possess mysterious wellsprings of energy. Rome was calling him again.

CHAPTER 9

❖

Writing Sonnets in the College: The Amorous Cardinal Bembo

Šipan Island, October 1559. Monsignor Ludovico Beccadelli exchanges a glance with his chaplain, Pellegrino Brocardo. The latter is making quick progress on the fresco: only the portraits of Reginald Pole and Jacopo Sadoleto are still missing. When the fresco is finished, an entire world of friendships, affection, and literary and religious passions will return to life on the wall of a small church on the island to which Monsignore has been exiled by the ferocious Paul IV. The fresco is to depict 'our MM. Contarino and Bembo, and Fracastoro and Sannazaro, and Navaiero, with Venice nearby, and among them our M. Michelangelo, who is alive and appears to be thinking'. On the walls of the small church, the main protagonists of Italian Evangelism would forever pursue their discussion of the season of spiritual renewal, when it was still possible to believe in a purified Church — a Church in which literature contributed to the perfecting of man, while art immortalised him through images of imperishable beauty. By 1559, however, all these men were either dead or banished or silenced. The new age was one of censorship, condemnation and contempt for poetry. A new generation of arrogant, vulgar censors and coarse guardians of the orthodoxy had risen; they condemned Bembo, the great Bembo, as a blasphemous sensualist, for scandalously describing the women he loved with adjectives that should properly by applied only to God. *Non est tolerandum!* His books deserved to be punished, if not banned.

In the years that followed Pietro's election as cardinal *in pectore*, in December 1538 (he effectively took up the position on 19 March of the following year), a tremendous cultural upheaval took place. Pietro had not yet been ordained at the time of his election, which was highly unusual; he took the vows only in December 1539. Giovan Pietro Carafa duly warned Paul III: 'Holy Father, we do not need men in our college who can write sonnets'. Carafa viewed faith as a constant struggle against the thousand-headed hydra of heresy: Lutherans, Calvinists, Anabaptists, Antitrinitarians, Evangelists, Nicodemites, apostates and free thinkers. He made sure the eyes and ears of the Inquisition were everywhere: with grasping hands it dug, probed, questioned, tortured, imprisoned, fined and purged.

Ludovico Beccadelli lays down his pen and rereads the last pages of his biography of Pietro, which he had finished over the summer. Pietro sauntered through life as if through a comedy, taking pains in the end to ensure that its final act was as praiseworthy as possible. And the comedy of his life unfolded on the most powerful stage of the world: the city of Venice. Twenty year earlier, in a letter to the pope's nephew Cardinal Alessandro Farnese, his main benefactor, Pietro defended himself against slanderers, bigots and *chietini*, as the disciples of the terrible Carafa, Cardinal of Chieti, were called:

> I refrain from complaining to your Reverence about those who slander me, since you must know how unfounded their criticisms are, given my advanced age. Praise God, I live as a man of experience should, aware that mistakes and trespasses tolerated in a young man cannot be forgiven in old age. I am a man, moreover, who has satisfied his appetite for all the variety this world has to offer, and is now taking honourable pains to end the comedy of his life in a praiseworthy manner. A comedy of which this great and populous city was both the theatre and the witness.

Monsignore Beccadelli's mind then skipped forwards to the final act of that happy comedy.

Rome, Palazzo Baldassini, 18 January 1547. Behind the white gate, a hushed silence enveloped the loggias and hallways of the grand palace designed by Antonio da Sangallo. On its walls and ceilings, the figures in the frescoes by Giovanni da Udine and Perin del Vaga, Raphael's favourite collaborators, seemed to have fallen silent: the philosophers were mute, as were the gods and the ancient Romans. In a darkened room, Pietro Bembo lay dying. He had been running a low fever for several days. Lucid as ever, he understood from the onset of the first symptoms that this time he would not recover. He spent his final days discussing spiritual questions, especially the benefits of our Lord Jesus Christ. The day before he died, he received a visit from the Cardinal Reginald Pole, a member of the *Spirituali*, a group of reformers intent on restoring the Church to its original purity and humility. Many of Pietro's friends belonged to this group, including his compatriot Cardinal Contarini, Sadoleto, Federico Fregoso, Michelangelo, Vittoria Colonna and the late Bishop of Fano, Cosimo Gheri, who was said to have died of shame at the age of twenty-four after being tied up and raped by the son of Pope Paul III, the terrible Pier Luigi Farnese. Soon Pope Paul IV Carafa and the running dogs of the Inquisition would destroy these men and women, reduce them to silence, imprison or hunt them down. Reginald lowered his legendary thick beard toward Pietro's face and whispered softly in his ear [Figure 28].

'Do you remember, Monsignore,' he reportedly said, 'the dream that our dear Cosimo dreamed before he died? Do you remember, Monsignore, that in his dream you and I were with Gasparo Contarini and poor Cosimo.' 'It was not a dream,' Pietro answered, 'but a vision.' He believed in signs and dreams. In a letter to Giovan Matteo in 1544, for instance, he mentioned a rumour in Venice, according to which he would one day succeed to the papacy: the position of Jupiter at the centre of the sky on the day of his birth left no room for doubt, at least not in the mind of the astrologer Federico Badoer. Similarly, during the Mass at which he received his cardinal's hat, he happened to read the call of Peter in the gospel ('I was called, like St Peter, with the words "Petre, sequere me." Those words surprised everyone present at that Mass'). And then there was the hermit who predicted that

Fig. 28. Sebastiano del Piombo, *Portrait of Cardinal Reginald Pole*, c. 1540, oil on canvas, 112 × 95 cm, Hermitage Museum, Saint Petersburg. © 2015. Photo Fine Art Images/Heritage Images/Scala, Florence

a Bishop of Gubbio would be elected pope. One cannot help wondering whether, at moments like these, Pietro recalled the dreams of his mother Elena and that day long ago when she begged him to stay away from the Rialto. We shall never know.

What we do know, however, is that when Ludovico Beccadelli, Pietro's biographer, wrote that before dying he was reflecting on the 'benefits of Christ', he was taking a considerable risk. Possibly a calculated risk, or one that he saw as necessary. Indeed, the phrase 'benefits of Christ' echoes the title of a small book, *Beneficio di Cristo*, published anonymously four years earlier (it was in fact written by a Benedictine monk, Don Benedetto Fontanini, with help from the great Humanist Marco Antonio Flaminio). It was a huge success, though its subversive implications were soon widely understood. It focused on the salvation offered to us by Christ's sacrifice and contended that man is saved not by his acts but by divine grace. This happened to be the central thesis of Lutheran theology. Such a position struck a blow at the very heart of the Roman Catholic system: if man was saved by faith alone, there was no longer any need for indulgences, prayers for the dead and the intercession of the clergy. In reality, the argument of *Beneficio di Cristo* was more nuanced, but at heart the question was the same. It became the article of faith of the *Spirituali*. Pietro was close to many members of that group, which included one of his closest friends and collaborators of the later years, Vittore Soranzo, who succeed him as Bishop of Bergamo and was twice judged by the Inquisition.

The meaning of Cosimo Gheri's vision is elucidated in a letter from Monsignore Beccadelli to Cosimo's brother, Filippo Gheri. Beccadelli describes the dream in greater detail and explains the hidden significance of the words whispered by Reginald Pole to the dying Pietro. In this dream, Cosimo is climbing a steep mountain covered in thorns in company of Pietro, Reginald Pole and Gasparo Contarini. At the top of the mountain is a field, encircled by a wall with barred windows. In the strange, discontinuous manner of dreams, Cosimo suddenly notices that he is alone. Looking through the windows, he sees his friends on the other side of the wall. He is trying in vain to open the door to join them, when a handsome old man with a kind countenance opens it and admits him to heaven. The meaning of the dream was too obvious to be circulated beyond a small group of close friends: man may exert himself all he wants with his works, but only by God's grace can he enter heaven. The words on the dying Bembo's lips were apparently none other than Luther's central thesis, echoed, with a few variations, by the *Beneficio di Cristo*.

The last years of Bembo's life unfolded in what was for him a new dimension, that of religion. The old Humanist, the poet of love, the idol of the courts, the man who took vows and broke them, who strove constantly to acquire new benefices and ecclesiastical revenues, only to bequeath them to his children or relatives, now seemed eager to steer his life in a more spiritual direction. In October 1539, he returned to Rome to continue his brilliant career in the Church. On 10 November of the same year, he was named Cardinal of San Ciriaco in Thermis. He acquired the titles of Cardinal of San Crisogono on 15 February 1542 and Cardinal of San Clemente on 17 October 1544. In the meantime, on 29 July 1541, he was appointed Bishop of Gubbio, though he was unable to celebrate his nomination, since it came shortly after the death of his friend Federico Fregoso. The latter position provided an opportunity to return to the Duchy of Urbino after an absence of thirty years, but Pietro waited until 1543 before moving to the small city of Gubbio, in Umbria. His stay there was brief, for he was named Bishop of Bergamo on 18 February 1544. He opted to send the faithful Vittore Soranzo to his new diocese in his place, with the title of Bishop Coadjutor, while he returned to the Curia in Rome.

Pietro's career required an astonishing amount of work for a man of his age, and it took its toll on him. After returning to Rome, he followed the pope to Bologna and Busseto in the summer of 1543 for a meeting with Charles V, similar to the one held by Paul III thirteen years prior. The emperor had convened a Diet in the German city of Speyer in 1542, but the meeting with the Protestant princes had been unsuccessful, and the rift between them had only widened as a result. The aim at Busseto was to discuss the possibility of a Council to resolve the divergences. The failure of the Diet had aggravated an already delicate situation: the emperor could no longer count on the support of the German princes against the King of France, François I, who had allied himself with Suleiman I. Meanwhile, the sultan's formidable admiral Barbarossa had secured an alarming maritime supremacy in the Mediterranean. This was certainly also discussed at Busseto. The pope asked Charles V to name his nephew Ottavio, who was married to the emperor's daughter Margaret of Austria, Duke of Milan. In this way, the ruthless old pope was attempting to establish a 'Farnesian' state in Italy; in 1545, he scandalously manoeuvred to detach the cities of Parma and Piacenza from the Papal States to give them to his son Pier Luigi.

Around the same time in Rome, between late 1542 and early 1543, with the same indomitable energy, another old man, Michelangelo, started work on two huge frescoes, measuring six by six metres, in the Vatican's Pauline Chapel, where the conclave assembled. This was an extraordinary challenge for a man of sixty with failing eyesight (his friend Vittoria Colonna gave him a pair of spectacles when he visited her in Viterbo in the summer of 1543, in the company of Pole, Flaminio and other members of the *Spirituali* who were regular visitors to her house), who, moreover, was physically deformed by the herculean labour of the vault of the Sistine Chapel and exhausted by the painting of its *Final Judgement*. Yet here he was, preparing to paint the *Conversion of St Paul* and the *Crucifixion of St Peter* [Figures 29–30]

These two scenes not only heralded an aesthetic revolution, but also contained a doctrinal subtext, for the writings of St Paul were especially popular among believers in justification by faith. Painting in a simple, unfussy style without narrative digressions, Michelangelo placed the bodies of both saints in an exclusive relationship to both Christ and the viewer by surrounding them with a crowd of feeble-looking figures representing the elect and the poor, who appear naked in their faith. Additionally, all references to Rome have disappeared.

Thus, in 1543, in the entourage of the terrible Paul III, Pietro and Michelangelo crossed paths. The artist lived for many years in exile in Rome, but never came to love the city. Pietro, meanwhile, was preparing to join him there for the last exile of his long, peripatetic life. He knew that he would never return to his house in

Fig. 29. Michelangelo, *Conversion of Saul*, 1542–45, fresco, Pauline Chapel, Vatican. © 2015 Photo Scala, Florence

Fig. 30. Michelangelo, *Crucifixion of St Peter*, 1545–50, fresco, Pauline Chapel, Vatican. © 2015 Photo Scala, Florence

Noniano, and asked for permission — which was granted — to make a last trip to Padua and Venice. He stayed in Venice until October, before moving to his diocese of Gubbio.

In spite of the increasingly heavy responsibilities he shouldered in those years of fierce ideological conflict on either side of the Alps, Pietro never forgot to play his role of prince of letters. It seems reasonable to assume that his sudden religious turn was motivated not only by ambition and a desire to advance his career in the Church, but also by sympathy, if not agreement, with the views of the *Spirituali*. Yet he continued to be active as a writer and poet — albeit in a manner very different from that of his friend Vittoria Colonna, who, around 1539–40, inaugurated a new era in poetry by combining Petrarchism with themes dear to the *Spirituali*. Pietro was fully aware of this shift, but he had neither the time nor the desire to explore a new poetic style, opting instead to retouch and develop what he had already written. Accordingly, in 1538 he published a second edition of the *Prose della volgar lingua*, while continuing to revise his poems and compose new ones. In 1543, he finished his history of Venice, and the following year started to translate it into the vernacular, an undertaking that took him two years.

And as if that were not enough, in 1537, he contrived to fall in love again with a noblewoman, Elisabetta Massolo, née Querini. Their relationship was most certainly platonic. Elisabetta was a charming woman and admired also by Pietro's friend Giovanni Della Casa; Titian painted her portrait. Pietro dedicated his edition of the history of Venice, published posthumously in 1552, to her. As usual, the relationship was both sentimental and literary. Elisabetta was highly educated, and Pietro often turned to her for advice. She was 'remarkable for her knowledge of literature, greatness of spirit and corporeal beauty.' To praise her in his sonnets, Pietro recycled a conceit previously applied to Lucrezia Borgia, describing her as 'the woman about whom one cannot say whether she is more beautiful or more learned'; she offered a 'precious aid to the spirit of my fragile life' (from the sonnet *Se mai ti piacque, Apollo, non indegno*). Moreover, she 'shows the way to heaven and teaches me how to avoid vulgarity' (in the sonnet *Quella che co' begli occhi par che invoglie*). Pietro repeatedly declared himself incapable of adequately describing her beauty, but the immaterial connotations of love are obvious in those sonnets; although they repeat many familiar themes from the *dolce stilnovo* and Book III of *Gli Asolani*, they are also full of real spiritual resonances. It is worth pointing out that, unlike *Gli Asolani*, they represent woman as capable of leading man in the direction of heaven.

There was also a practical aspect to their relationship. For example, Pietro introduced Elisabetta's son Piero to his friend Gregorio Cortese, abbot of San Benedetto Po near Mantua, after the young man impetuously murdered his new bride on their wedding night. Piero later took the Benedictine habit and devoted himself to the study of philosophy and theology. On becoming a monk, he changed his name to Lorenzo, which also happened to be the name of his father.

The elder Lorenzo commissioned a painting of the Martyrdom of St Lawrence for the Church of I Gesuiti in Venice from Titian [Figure 31] to hang above the tomb designed to receive the remains of Lorenzo, Elisabetta and their daughter. Although

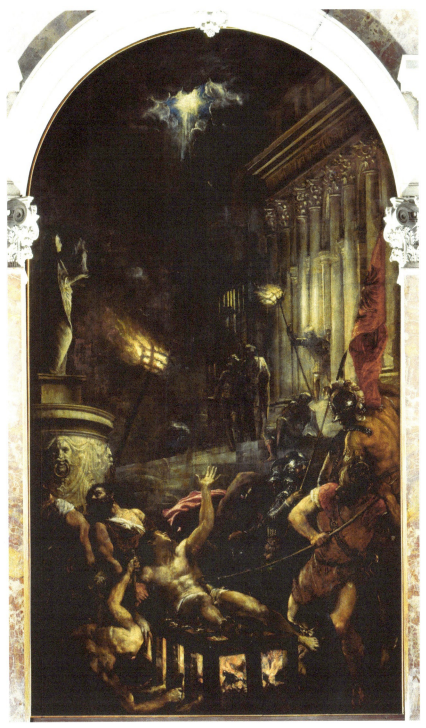

Fig. 31. Titian, *Martyrdom of St Lawrence*, *c.* 1548–57, oil on canvas, 493 × 277 cm, church of Santa Maria Assunta dei Gesuiti, Venice. © 2015 Cameraphoto/Scala, Florence

the painting was ordered in 1548, Elisabetta was still asking the artist to finish it as late as 1557. This work reflects a deep familiarity with the Greco-Roman world, as shown by the numerous references it contains (a statue of Vesta holding a Victory on the left and a colonnade on the right, perhaps the Roman temple of Antoninus and Faustina or that of Mars Ultor). This painting stands out for both its novel nocturnal setting and the highly unorthodox iconography of the saint, as if its intention was to emphasise the commissioner's disagreement with the many heresies that were brewing in Venice at the time. Such an intellectual work of art was probably not devised by Lorenzo but by Elisabetta and her circle of intellectuals. Elisabetta and Pietro broke of relations when he left for Rome. Around late September 1539, he sent her a short letter accompanying a portrait of himself, in which he asked her to content herself with seeing him as he had become, 'hunched and withered' (or 'bearded and old' in a different version).

These were exhausting years on every front for Pietro. Elisabetta was not the only one with family troubles; Pietro also had his share of bad luck. The beloved Cola Bruno died in 1542, as mentioned earlier. The following year, he had to organise the marriage of his daughter Elena to Pietro Gradenigo. A wedding — and its ensuing expense — was not the sort of event that Pietro looked forward to. Less than a month after the wedding, his new son-in-law started to stir up trouble, demanding that Pietro hand over to him the income of Villa Bozza. To make matters worse, Elena ungratefully sided with her husband against her father, although the latter had been generous with gifts of money and chattels. Pietro sorrowfully resolved to ban her from his house: 'Elena, I wish you to know that you have acted disgracefully, and that you should not be so quick to forget the love I have so often shown you, as well as your obligations toward me, nor should you turn your mind against me, your father. I hear that you plan to come to Padua at Christmas, but I must warn you that you shall not set foot in my house so long as I am still of this world'. Nonetheless, in April 1544, he agreed to a reconciliation after she begged him for forgiveness. Meanwhile, despite the birth of a son, Paolo, Gradenigo had started to be unfaithful, or so Pietro hinted in two letters to Giovan Matteo Bembo, dated 20 and 28 June 1545. A letter dated 15 August no longer leaves any room for doubt: 'if Elena believes that Pietro Gradenigo no longer visits his darling mistress, all the better for her, though it isn't true; please tell her on my behalf that the best course of action is not to worry or to speak about it, and to be always calm and modest, not proud or haughty'.

However, Pietro worried most about his son Torquato. He was responsible for carrying on the family line and would one day inherit the house, the library, the collection of antiquities, the whole tangled mess of possessions and passions which Pietro and his father Bernardo had in common, despite their differences. Pietro asked Cola Bruno to show his relics and medals to his son in the hope of arousing in him some interest in this legacy. Torquato was not stupid, but he was lazy and apathetic. On 26 December 1540, Pietro scolded him:

> 'Torquato, my son, [...] I believe you could certainly study if you wanted, for you have all the necessary qualities. But you never apply yourself, and instead lose yourself in your games, devoting very little time to your studies. Wake up! Don't allow yourself to fall asleep at such an important time in your life!

> Riding, which you love so much, and games and distractions, deliver only the empty pleasure of the moment. When that is gone, nothing remains.

But his warning fell on deaf ears. In July 1542, Pietro threatened to disinherit Torquato:

> If, during the next two years, you fail to make any significant progress in your studies, you shall receive no part of my inheritance: neither the house in Padua, nor my studio, nor any of the things I own here and there, nor any share of the objects in this house, which are worth several thousand ducats: not a single plate or piece of string.

Two years later, Pietro declared that he planned to leave everything to his daughter Elena, including the house, the studio and two thousand *écus* (letter to Girolamo Querini, 15 July 1544). By 1546 he seemed to have come to terms with the fact that his son, then twenty-one, would never live up to his expectations. The young man — possibly with the complicity of his tutor — sent him detailed reports on the progress he was making in his studies. But Pietro knew he was lying:

> Torquato, it costs me nothing to praise you for what you tell me you have accomplished. And I would happily praise you if I were certain it was true. But you have given me reason to deplore your lack of application in your studies for so long that, even if M. Felice confirms what you tell me, I have difficulty believing either of you. I know that you seize every opportunity to shirk your duties, and that you are weak when it comes to learning virtue and doctrine. And this is not the fruit of a heart as great as I would wish yours to be. And I know that if you deceive me, you deceive yourself even more.

If Torquato was lazy, Elena was only too eager to learn and, at the age of thirteen, had to be warned not to study certain arts, in order to preserve her reputation. In December 1541, her father wrote:

> Regarding the permission you seek to learn the monocord, I am trying to explain what you cannot understand at your age, namely, that playing an instrument is a pursuit suitable only for vain, frivolous women. Whereas I wish you to be the most sober, chaste and modest of women. Besides, if you play poorly, music will bring you little pleasure and great shame. Give up this futile idea, and be instead humble, kind, well behaved and obedient. And if your friends beg you to learn to play for their enjoyment, you must tell them that you do not want to provoke their amusement at the expense of your shame. Be content with reading and needlework, which are valuable skills if you master them well.

Where had he gone, that passionate young man who once climbed up a ladder to Maria Savorgnan's window? Where was the lover of Lucrezia Borgia, the charming poet of the courts at which people danced, sang, performed plays and read poems that urged them to enjoy love and youth? Pietro had grown old. The years weighed heavily upon him and, sensing the arrival of a season full of alarming portents, he repeatedly tried to steer his children on the path of virtue. His indomitable spirit kept him going until the last; his final letters show him still fully engaged in the management of his affairs and the Badia di Villanova, or intervening with the doge in favour of his son-in-law's father. As if to prove the breadth of his learning, which over the years encompassed Latin, Greek, Provençal, Hebrew and many other more abstruse fields of knowledge, he interceded with the Archbishop of Cyprus in favour of the 'Indian brothers who are in Rome', arranging to provide this community of Ethiopian monks with a manuscript of the Epistles of St Paul, with a view to an edition of the New Testament in Ge'ez, the ancient language of Ethiopia.

Everything was finally ready. Lulled by Pole's soft whisper, Pietro closed his eyes and started his final journey. He walked slowly, Cola Bruno and the good Molza by his side. Fregoso and Contarini descended from the hierarchies of angels to benevolently escort him. A long row of friends was waiting for him. He no longer felt the fever tremors. His legs were as strong as they had been many years ago on the Rialto. His eyes saw clearly again and he rejoiced in the brilliance of the celestial firmament, which was like the light that sometimes enfolds the basin of San Marco and the island of San Giorgio where the lagoon meets the open sea. Heavenly melodies enveloped him, then immediately ceased in sign of astonished admiration. Reunited with his friends, honoured and praised, the king of letters, the supreme cardinal, took his place on a chair 'covered in scarlet under a green laurel', a chair that had been readied for him for all eternity: 'ab eterno preparata'. Pietro Bembo was, now and forever, what Heaven had decreed he should be. During his lifetime, his house was a 'public temple open onto the world', in which he 'sat in a glory worthy of Apollo'. Now, casting off his mortal remains and earthly illusions, he sat in the glory of the holy of holies, in the eternal temple of truth, where

> 'Day does not run towards night'.

BIBLIOGRAPHICAL NOTE

Given the nature and intended audience of this book, I have decided not to burden the text with numerous and tedious footnotes. Nevertheless, I thought it was important to provide readers with a general orientation to the literature on Pietro Bembo and the sources used in preparing this book, as well as the sources from which the many quotations of Bembo's works were drawn.

Translator's note: For the English translation, Bembo's writings are quoted from existing translations whenever possible (see bibliographical references below); in all other cases they are the translator's own.

Works by Bembo

Correspondence

Pietro Bembo, *Lettere*, edited by Ernesto Travi (Bologna: Commissione per i testi di lingua, 1987–93) (hereafter *Lettere*; letters are numbered sequentially).
Letters addressed to Pietro Bembo: *Delle lettere da diversi re, et principi, et cardinali, et altri huomini dotti a mons: Pietro Bembo scritte [...]* (Venice: Fra. Sansovino et compagni, MDLX); facsimile edition edited by Daria Perocco (Sala Bolognese: Forni, 1985).
Pietro Bembo and Maria Savorgnan: Maria Savorgnan–Pietro Bembo, *Carteggio d'amore (1500–1501)*, edited by Carlo Dionisotti (Florence: Le Monnier, 1950).
Pietro Bembo's correspondence with Lucrezia Borgia: *The Prettiest Love Letters in the World: Letters between Lucrezia Borgia and Pietro Bembo 1503 to 1519*, translated and preface by Hugh Shankland (Boston, MA: David R. Godine, 1987); P. Bembo–L. Borgia, *La grande fiamma: Lettere 1502–1517*, edited by Giulia Raboni (Milan: Archinto, 2002).

Other Works

De Ætna and the Latin poems: P. Bembo, *Lyric poetry, Etna*, edited and translated by Mary P. Chatfield (Cambridge, MA, and London: Harvard University Press, 2005).
De Urbini Ducibus: Italian–Latin bilingual edition, Pietro Bembo, *I Duchi di Urbino: De Urbini Ducibus Liber*, edited with a translation and a commentary by Valentina Marchesi (Bologna: I libri di Emil, 2010); vernacular version: Pietro Bembo, *Volgarizzamento des Dialogs De Guido Ubaldo Feretrio deque Elisabetha Gonzagia Urbini ducibus*, edited with a commentary by Maria Lutz (Geneva: Droz, 1980).
Gli Asolani: English translation, *Pietro Bembo's Gli Asolani*, translated by Rudolf B. Gottfried (Bloomington: Indiana University Press, 1954); Italian, Pietro Bembo, *Gli Asolani*, critical edition by Giorgio Dilemmi (Florence: Presso l'Accademia della Crusca, 1991) and Pietro Bembo, *Gli Asolani / Les Azolains*, translated and presented by Marie Françoise Piéjus, introduction by Mario Pozzi, text and notes by Carlo Dionisotti (Paris: Les Belles Lettres, 2006).
Historiæ Venetæ: Pietro Bembo, *History of Venice*, edited and translated by Robert W. Ulery Jr. (Cambridge, MA, and London: Harvard University Press, 2007); the Latin text was

first printed in Venice (apud Aldi filios, 1551) and Paris (Michael Vascosanus, 1551); first vernacular edition, *Della historia vinitiana* (Venice: appresso Gualtiero Scotto, 1552) (= *Historia vinitiana*), which was censored; a faithful edition was published only in 1790, *Della istoria viniziana di m. Pietro Bembo cardinale da lui volgarizzata libri dodici: Ora per la prima volta secondo l'originale pubblicati* (Venice: per Antonio Zatta, 1790).

Leggi della compagnia degli amici: Pietro Bembo, *Prose e rime*, edited by Carlo Dionisotti (Turin: U.T.E.T., 1966), pp. 699–703 (Hereafter *Prose e rime*).

Motti: Pietro Bembo, *Motti*, edited by Vittorio Cian, preface by Alessandro Gnocchi, notes and index by Giulia Raboni (Milan: Sylvestre Bonnard, 2007). Vittorio Cian's original 1888 edition with a new introduction and indexes.

Oratio pro litteris græcis and *De Virgilii Culice*: Latin–English bilingual edition established by Nigel G. Wilson (Messina: Centro interdipartimentale di Studi umanistici, 2003). I was able to consult the first edition of *De Virgilii*: *Petri Bembi ad Herculem Strotium de Virgilii Culice et Terentii fabulis liber* (Venice: Per Io. Ant. eiusque fratres Sabios, Ann. MDXXX).

Prose della volgar lingua: Pietro Bembo, *Prose e rime*, edited by Carlo Dionisotti (Turin: U.T.E.T., 1966), pp. 73–309; see also the interesting edition comparing the first edition to the autograph MS Vat. Lat. 3210, Pietro Bembo, *Prose della volgar lingua: L'editio princeps del 1525 riscontrata con l'autografo Vaticano latino 3210*, critical edition by Claudio Vela (Bologna: C.L.U.E.B., 2001).

Sogno and *Rime*: Pietro Bembo, *Rime*, edited by Andrea Donnini (Rome: Salerno Editrice, 2008).

Stanze: Pietro Bembo, *Stanze*, edited by Alessandro Gnocchi (Florence: Società Editrice Fiorentina, 2003).

Reference works

Carlo Dionisotti's important collection of essays, *Scritti sul Bembo*, edited by Claudio Vela (Turin: Einaudi, 2002); Vittorio Cian's seminal research on Bembo, especially *Un decennio della vita di M. Pietro Bembo (1521–1531): Appunti biografici e saggio di studi sul Bembo* (Turin: Loescher, 1885), and *Un medaglione del Rinascimento: Cola Bruno messinese e le sue relazioni con Pietro Bembo (1480 c.– 1542)* (Florence: Sansoni, 1901); a generally useful biography of Bembo despite some inaccuracies: Carol Kidwell, *Pietro Bembo: Lover, Linguist, Cardinal* (Montreal: McGill–Queen's University Press, 2004). Other recent studies include: Massimo Danzi, *La biblioteca del cardinal Pietro Bembo* (Geneva: Droz, 2005); *Pietro Bembo e l'invenzione del Rinascimento*, exhibition catalogue, Padua, Palazzo del Monte di Pietà, 2 February–19 May 2013, edited by Guido Beltramini, Davide Gasparotto, Adolfo Tura (Venice: Marsilio, 2013); *Pietro Bembo e le arti*, edited by Guido Beltramini, Howard Burns e Davide Gasparotto (Venice: Marsilio, 2013).

Prologue

Ludovico Beccadelli is quoted from *Vita del cardinale Pietro Bembo*, in *Monumenti di varia letteratura tratti dai manoscritti di monsignor Lodovico Beccadelli* vol. I, p. II (Bologna: nell'Instituto Nazionale, 1799), pp. 223–52 (p. 246). Della Casa is quoted from Giovanni Della Casa, *Vita di Pietro Bembo*, edited and translated by Antonino Sole (Turin: Fògola, 1997), pp. 116, 115, 121 (Latin text on pp. 52, 50, 56).

Chapter 1

Cellini is quoted from Benvenuto Cellini, *Vita*, edited by Ettore Camesasca (Milan: Rizzoli, 2004), pp. 320–21. Varchi's definition appears in the *Orazione* for Bembo's death, in *Delle Orazioni volgarmente scritte da diversi uomini illustri raccolte per M. Francesco Sansovino*

[...] (Lyon: Appresso Giuseppe e Vincenzo Lanais, 1741), pp. 97–114 (p. 108). Beccadelli is quoted from *Vita*, cit., p. 246. English translations of the sonnets to Lucrezia are from *The Prettiest Love Letters*, cit. VII, and translator's own respectively. The sonnets by Querini, Tiepolo and Ariosto appear in Alessandro Gnocchi, 'Tommaso Giustiniani, Ludovico Ariosto e la Compagnia degli amici', *Studi di Filologia italiana*, 67 (1999), 277–93.

Chapter 2

The sonnet in Bembo's honour appears in Massimo Danzi, 'Novità su Michele Marullo e Pietro Bembo', *Rinascimento*, 30 (1990), pp. 205–33 (pp. 226–27, more generally pp. 225–28). Augurelli's poem appears in his *Carminum libri*, published in 1491 and 1501, and by Aldo Manuzio in Venice, April 1505; poem at c. oiii^{r-v}.

On the relationship between Pietro Bembo and the Medici, see Vittorio Cian, 'Per Bernardo Bembo: Le sue relazioni coi Medici', in *Giornale storico della Letteratura italiana*, 88 (1896), 348–64 (Bernardo Bembo's letter is quoted on p. 359); and Nella Giannetto, *Bernardo Bembo: Umanista e politico veneziano* (Florence: Olschki, 1985).

Quotation from *Historia vinitiana*, c. 1^v.

Della Casa is quoted from *Vita*, cit., p. 120 (Latin text on pp. 55–56). The letter to Ramusio appears in *Lettere*, II, n. 637, pp. 329–30.

Manuzio's dedication for Lascaris's *Erotemata* appears in a collection of the great humanist's dedications: *Aldo Manuzio editore: dediche, prefazioni, note ai testi*, introduction by Carlo Dionisotti, Latin text, commentary and notes by Giovanni Orlandi (Milan: Il Polifilo, 1975), vol. II, p. 3; another interesting study on Manuzio is Carlo Dionisotti, *Aldo Manuzio umanista e editore* (Milan: Il Polifilo, 1995).

Guicciardini quotation: Francesco Guicciardini, *Storia d'Italia*, edited by Silvana Seidel Menchi (Turin: Einaudi, 1971), pp. 1–2. English translation: Id., *The History of Italy*, translated, edited, with notes and an introduction by Sidney Alexander (Princeton, NJ: Princeton University Press, 1984 [first edn. 1969]), pp. 3–4.

The 1535 testament is quoted in Cian, *Un decennio...*, op. cit., pp. 201–02.

Chapter 3

A modern edition of Leoniceno's work: Niccolò Leoniceno, *De Plinii in medicina erroribus*, edited by Loris Premuda (Rome: Edizione de 'Il Giardino di Esculapio', 1958).

Quotations from *Prose* appear in *Prose e rime*, pp. 82–83.

Aviso a gli lettori of 1501, in *Aldo Manuzio editore*, cit., pp. 52–55, quotations appear on p. 54 and pp. 54–55.

The two commentaries by Antonio da Canal appear in Gino Belloni, 'Antonio da Canal e polemiche aldine', in Id., *Laura tra Petrarca e Bembo: Studi sul commento umanistico-rinascimentale al 'Canzoniere'* (Padua: Antenore, 1992), pp. 96–119, quotations on pp. 103, 106.

The discussion of Bembo, Ermolao and the aspirations of the new Venetian humanism are broadly indebted to the pioneering work of Vittore Branca, 'L'eredità barbariana nel Bembo: L'umanesimo volgare e la "Respublica litteraria"', in Id., *La sapienza civile: Studi sull'Umanesimo a Venezia* (Florence: Olschki, 1999), pp. 129–44, quotation on p. 143.

Letter to Tebaldeo: *Lettere*, II, n. 803, pp. 455–56, quotation on p. 455.

The quotation from *De Virgilii* is from the above-cited edition, c. av^v. Michiel is quoted in Francesco Paolo Di Teodoro, *Raffaello, Baldassar Castiglione e la 'Lettera a Leone X': Con *l'aggiunta di due saggi raffaelleschi* (Bologna: Minerva, 2003), pp. 260–61; the quotations from *Lettera* are on pp. 176–77, 179.

Chapter 4

All quotations from Pietro and Maria Savorgnan's correspondence are from *Carteggio d'amore*, cit., pp. 20, 44, 6–7, 13, 19, 22, 13, 61, 9, 79, 66, 4, 73–74, 135, 126–27, 11, 65, 90, 23, 25, 28, 32, 58, 101, 92.

Dionisotti is quoted in *Scritti sul Bembo*, p. 13.

Regarding Maria Savorgnan, see Roberto Zapperi, 'Chi era Maria Savorgnan?' *Studi veneziani*, 44 (2005), 281–83; Zapperi identifies her as Maria Griffoni, daughter of Matteo Griffoni, of Sant'Angelo in Vado, Marche, commander of the Serenissima.

The descriptions of Lucrezia's arrival appear in *Lucrezia Borgia in Ferrara sposa a don Alfonso d'Este: Memorie storiche estratte dalla Cronaca ferrarese di Bernardino Zambotto [...]* (Ferrara: Domenico Taddei tipografo editore, 1867), pp. 40–41, 21, 20, 39–40.

Ariosto's eclogue appears in Ludovico Ariosto, *Rime*, edited by Stefano Bianchi (Milan: Rizzoli, 1992), pp. 187–98: the passage quoted is on p. 197.

The letters to and from Lucrezia Borgia appear in *La grande fiamma*, cit. pp. 31, 32, 33, 80, 39, 41, 45, 48, 50, 57–58, 59–60; English translations are from *The Prettiest Love Letters*, cit. pp. IX, X, XI, V, XVI, XIX, XXX.

Letter from Bembo to Isabella d'Este: *Lettere*, I, n. 206, p. 194. Regarding their relationship, see Vittorio Cian, 'Pietro Bembo e Isabella d'Este Gonzaga: Note e documenti,' *Giornale storico della Letteratura italiana*, 9 (1887), 81–136; the *bussolino* is mentioned on p. 119.

Sermini's letter, Alessandro Luzio–Rodolfo Renier, *La coltura e le relazioni letterarie di Isabella d'Este Gonzaga*, edited by Simone Albonico, introduction by Giovanni Agosti (Milan: Sylvestre Bonnard, 2005), p. 164.

The quotation from the Pasquino, *Lettera* in ms. Ottob. Lat. 2812, Biblioteca Apostolica Vaticana, c. 6^v.

Letter to Tomarozzo: *Lettere*, IV, n. 2347, pp. 430–31 (p. 431).

Chapter 5

Quotations from *Gli Asolani* are on pp. 8, 13, 14, 182, 184, 189, 185.

The passage about the king of the Fortunate Isles appears in *Historia vinitiana*, c. 44^v.

Regarding Bembo in the *Cortegiano*, see Guido Arbizzoni, *L'ordine e la persuasione: Pietro Bembo personaggio nel 'Cortegiano'* (Urbino: Quattroventi, 1983).

Regarding *Gli Asolani* as a source of poetic imagery, see Maiko Favaro, *L'ospite preziosa: Presenza della lirica nei trattati d'amore del '500 e del primo '600* (Lucca: Pacini Fazzi, 2013).

An interesting reading of *Gli Asolani* in the context of the Renaissance art of portraiture is provided by Lina Bolzoni, *Il cuore di cristallo: Ragionamenti d'amore, poesia e ritratto nel Rinascimento* (Turin: Einaudi, 2010).

Letter to Bibbiena: *Lettere*, I, n. 210, pp. 196–97 (p. 197).

The quotation from *Piacevoli notti* appears in Giovan Francesco Straparola, *Le piacevoli notti*, edited by Donato Pirovano (Rome: Salerno Editrice, 2000), vol. I, pp. 5–10.

Chapter 6

The quotation from *Cortegiano* appears in Baldassarre Castiglione, *Il libro del Cortegiano*, edited by Amedeo Quondam (Milan: Mondadori, 2002), p. 400.

The quotation from the letter to Henry VIII appears in Baldassarre Castiglione, *Lettera a Enrico VIII*, in Id., *Lettere*, edited by Guido La Rocca, vol. I (Milan: Mondadori, 1978), pp. 162–98 (p. 190–91). Another version in Latin is reproduced in Castiglione, *Vita di Guidubaldo duca di Urbino*, edited by Uberto Motta (Rome: Salerno Editrice, 2006).

Regarding Bembo's ecclesiastical benefices and his Roman period more generally, see Alessandro Ferrajoli's seminal essay of 1914, 'Pietro Bembo', reprinted in *Il ruolo della corte di Leone X*, edited by Vincenzo De Caprio (Rome: Bulzoni, 1984), pp. 247–332 (pp. 255–80).

Documents concerning work on the Villa Imperiale are reproduced in Giorgio Gronau, *Documenti artistici urbinati* (Urbino: Accademia Raffaello, 2011), pp. 128–29 (facsimile of the 1936 edition, Florence: Sansoni).

Letter to Leonardi: *Lettere*, III, n. 1506, pp. 451–52 (p. 451).

Letter to Elisabetta and Emilia: *Lettere*, II, n. 231, pp. 216–20 (p. 219).

The anecdote relating Pietro's supposed love for Elisabetta appears in the second annex to Vittorio Cian's edition of the *Motti*, under the title 'Il Bembo e i giuochi alla Corte d'Urbino', pp. 87–89 (pp. 88–89); the original source is a sixteenth-century commentary of Bembo's poetry by Teodoro Amayden, Vatican Library ms. *Vat. Lat. 8825*.

Regarding the *Motti* and *Stanze*, see also Elisa Curti, *Tra due secoli: Per il tirocinio letterario di Pietro Bembo* (Bologna: Gedit, 2006), pp. 185–201 and 151–68.

The quotation about Francesco Maria Della Rovere is from Fabrizio Biferali, *Tiziano: Il genio e il potere* (Rome-Bari: Laterza, 2011), p. 128.

The 'Montefeltro form' of the *Rime* appears in Claudio Vela, 'Il primo canzoniere del Bembo (ms. Marc. It. IX 143)', *Studi di Filologia italiana*, 46 (1998), 163–251; the quotation from the dedication ballad is on p. 209.

Quotations from *Tirsi*: Claudio Vela, 'Il *Tirsi* di Baldassar Castiglione e Cesare Gonzaga', in *La poesia pastorale nel Rinascimento*, edited by Stefano Carrai (Padua: Antenore, 1998), pp. 245–92 (p. 285).

Quotations from *Stanze*: Bembo, *Stanze*, cit., pp. 67, 69, 79, 3.

Quotations from *De Urbini ducibus* from Bembo, *I Duchi di Urbino*, cit., pp. 159, 171–73, 179, 187.

Chapter 7

Quotation on the *Galatea* from Antonio Forcellino, *Raffaello: Una vita felice* (Rome-Bari: Laterza, 2009), p. 198.

Two letters to Bibbiena: *Lettere*, II, n. 368, pp. 112–14 (p. 114), and n. 371, p. 117.

Raphael's epitaph is quoted in Stefano Pagliaroli, 'L'epitaffio di Pietro Bembo per Raffaello', in *Pietro Bembo e l'invenzione del Rinascimento*, cit., pp. 292–99 (p. 292).

Letter to Gritti: *Lettere*, II, n. 358, pp. 102–06 (p. 103).

Letter about Bembo's illness: *Lettere*, II, n. 388, pp. 130–31 (p. 130).

Letter to Bibbiena: *Lettere*, II, n. 392, pp. 133–38 (pp. 133, 134–35).

The 'Pasquinata' appears in Pietro Aretino, *Operette politiche e satiriche*, vol. II, edited by Marco Faini (Rome: Salerno Editrice, 2012), p. 84.

Chapter 8

Aretino's sonnet: Aretino, *Operette politiche e satiriche*, cit., pp. 206–07.

Aretino's letters: Pietro Aretino, *Lettere*, edited by Paolo Procaccioli (Rome: Salerno, 1997–), vol. I (1997), p. 195; vol. VI (2002), p. 200; and vol. I, p. 364, 502–03.

Berni's sonnet: Francesco Berni, *Rime*, edited by Danilo Romei (Milan: Mursia, 1985), pp. 99–100 (p. 99).

Letters to Giberti: *Lettere*, II, n. 812, pp. 462–64 (pp. 463–64) and n. 845, pp. 488–90 (p. 490).

The Berni text: *Rime*, cit., pp. 11–115 (pp. 112 and 115).

Letter to Soranzo: *Lettere*, III, n. 1167, pp. 194–95.

Pietro's lament on the death of his friends appears in a letter to Giovan Matteo Bembo, *Lettere*, III, n. 966, p. 38.

Letter to Gritti: *Lettere*, n. 1267, pp. 270–71.

Letter to the Council of Ten: *Lettere*, n. 1275, p. 275.

Chapter 9

Letter from Beccadelli to Carlo Gualteruzzi of Ragusa (Dalmatia), 26 October 1559: Gigliola Fragnito, 'L'ultima visione: Il congedo di Pietro Bembo', in Id., *In museo e in villa: Saggi sul rinascimento perduto* (Venice: Arsenale, 1988), pp. 29–64 (p. 63); Giovan Pietro Carafa's reported words are on p. 29.

Letter to Farnese, 28 December 1538: *Lettere*, IV, n. 2002, pp. 166–67 (p. 167).

Letter to Giovan Matteo Bembo about calling: *Lettere*, IV, n. 2406, pp. 479–80 (p. 480).

Regarding Bembo as cardinal, see Massimo Firpo, 'Il cardinale Pietro Bembo', in *Pietro Bembo e le arti*, cit., pp. 23–36.

Regarding Soranzo, see Massimo Firpo, *Vittore Soranzo vescovo ed eretico: Riforma della Chiesa e Inquisizione nell'Italia del Cinquecento* (Rome-Bari: Laterza, 2006).

The description of Elisabetta appears in *Notizie istorico-critiche intorno la vita, e le opere degli scrittori viniziani, Raccolte, esaminate e distese da f. Giovanni degli Agostini [...]*, vol. II (Venice: presso Simone Occhi, 1754), p. 574.

Letter to Massola about sending the portrait: *Lettere*, IV, n. 2125, pp. 261–62 (p. 262).

Regarding Gregorio Cortese, see Gigliola Fragnito, *Il cardinal Gregorio Cortese nella crisi religiosa del Cinquecento* (Rome: Abbazia di San Paolo, 1983), and Massimo Zaggia, *Tra Mantova e la Sicilia nel Cinquecento*, 3 vols (Florence: Olschki, 2003).

Letters regarding Torquato and Elena: *Lettere*, IV, n. 2395, p. 469; n. 2491, p. 536; n. 2226, pp. 337–38; n. 2339, pp. 424–25 (p. 424); n. 2558, p. 585; n. 2303, pp. 398–99 (p. 398).

The reconstruction of Bembo's relationship with his sons is based on Danzi, *La biblioteca del cardinal Pietro Bembo*, cit., pp. 48–56.

Letter to the Archbishop of Cyprus Livio Podocataro (4 December 1546): *Lettere*, IV, n. 2577, p. 598.

Regarding the aspects of Bembo's culture mentioned in this chapter, see Pierre De Nolhac, *La bibliothèque de Fulvio Orsini: Contributions à l'histoire des collections d'Italie et à l'étude de la Renaissance* (Paris: Vieweg, 1887) and Danzi, *La biblioteca del cardinal Pietro Bembo*, cit. pp. 87–100.

The final section paraphrases Varchi's funeral oration, *Orazione*, cit.; quotations from pp. 111, 108–09. The final verse is from the song for the death of Pietro's brother Carlo, *Alma cortese, che dal mondo errante* (v. 164).

INDEX

Adrian VI, pope, *see* Florisz, Adriaan
Agosti, Giovanni 120
Alberti, Leon Battista 21, 29, 40, 92
Albonico, Simone 120
Alexander VI, pope, *see* Borgia, Rodrigo
Alexander, Sidney 119
Alighieri, Dante 18, 20, 30–33, 46, 57, 79, 92
Amaseo, Romolo Quirino 101
Amayden (Ameyden), Teodoro 121
Ambrogini, Angelo 17–19, 26, 36
Anjou, family 26
Anthony, saint 60
Anthony Abbott, saint 65
Antonio di Puccio Pisano 30
Apelles 92
Aragon, family 26
Aragon, Alfonso d', duke of Bisceglie 52
Aragon, Alfonso II d' 26
Aragon, Ferdinando (Ferrante) d' 16, 59
Aragon, Ferdinando II d' 72
Aragon, Isabella d' 26
Arbizzoni, Guido 120
Aretino, Pietro 4, 8, 79, 89, 94, 99–100, 121–22
Ariosto, Ludovico 4, 14, 30, 52, 119–20
Aristotle 29, 36
Arme, Francesco dall' 99
Augurelli, Giovanni Aurelio 17, 119

Badoer, Federico 106
Baldinelli, Ubaldino 100
Barbaro, Ermolao 22, 25–26, 29, 36–37, 119
Barbarossa see Khayr al-Dīn
Barbo, Paolo 37
Bartolomeo Veneto 48–49
Beccadelli, Ludovico 4, 27, 105–06, 108, 118–19, 122
Belli, Valerio 7, 8, 9
Bellini, Gentile 60, 63
Bellini, Giovanni 57
Belloni, Gino 119
Beltramini, Guido 118
Beltramo, Ferrier 68
Bembo, Antonio 68
Bembo, Bartolomeo 103
Bembo, Bernardo 1, 9, 16–18, 20–22, 26, 29, 31, 33, 36, 64, 66, 82, 93, 114, 119
Bembo, Carlo (brother of Pietro) 7, 56, 72, 78, 97, 122
Bembo, Carlo (nephew of Pietro) 103
Bembo, Elena 10, 27, 95, 103, 114–15, 122

Bembo, Giovan Matteo 93–94, 103, 106, 114, 122
Bembo, Lucilio 10, 95, 103
Bembo, Marcella 93–94
Bembo, Pietro:
   Benacus 98, 100
   De Ætna 23–26, 31–32, 36, 66, 99
   De corruptis poetarum locis 37
   De imitatione 36, 99
   De Urbini ducibus 82, 99
   De Virgilii Culice et Terentii fabulis 37, 99
   Edition of Petrarch's *Cose volgari* 31–33
   Edition of Dante's *Commedia* 31, 33
      Gli Asolani 4, 13, 30–31, 39, 46–47, 55, 60–61, 64, 66–68, 70, 77, 99, 112
      History of Venice 22, 66, 112
      Leggi della Compagnia degli Amici 13, 14, 67
      Motti 72, 79
      Oratio pro litteris græcis 25
      Prose della volgar lingua 21, 31–32, 47, 72, 82, 92–93, 95–99, 112
      Rime 78, 84, 99
      Sarca 98
      Sogno 18, 20, 22, 26
      Stanze 72, 78, 82
Bembo, Torquato 10, 27, 95, 103, 114–15, 122
Benci, Ginevra de' 21, 64
Bernardino 44
Bernardino di Betto Betti 53
Berni, Francesco 100, 102, 122
Beroaldo, Filippo 26, 82–83
Berva, Moreno ix
Bessarione, Basilio 22–23
Bevazzano (Beazzano), Agostino 89, 91
Bianchi, Stefano 120
Bibbiena *see* Dovizi da Bibbiena, Bernardo
Biferali, Fabrizio 121
Bilhères-Lagraulas, Jean de 89
Boccaccio, Giovanni 57, 92
Boiardo, Matteo Maria 30
Bolzoni, Lina 120
Bonasone, Giulio 11
Borgia, family 48, 50, 53
Borgia, Cesare (Valentino) 50, 53, 71, 82
Borgia, Lucrezia, 5, 14, 30, 48, 50–53, 55–58, 64, 71, 82, 95, 112, 115, 117, 119–20
Borgia, Rodrigo 48, 50, 71, 88
Bramante, Donato 89
Branca, Vittore 119

Brevio, Giovanni 100
Brocardo, Antonio 99–100
Brocardo, Pellegrino 105
Bruno, Cola 27, 44–45, 95, 99, 103, 114, 116, 118
Buonaccorsi, Pietro 106
Buonarroti, Michelangelo 66, 89–90, 92, 104–06, 109–11
Burns, Howard 118

Cagnola, Nicolò 50
Camesasca, Ettore 118
Campagnola, Giulio 66
Canal, Antonio da 32, 119
Canossa, Ludovico da 76
Cappello, Bernardo 68
Cappello, Francesco 66
Caracalla 7
Carafa, Giovan Pietro 105–06, 122
Casali, Giambattista 68
Castiglione, Baldassarre 14, 39–40, 64, 67, 71, 73, 76–77, 88–89, 91–92, 99, 101–02, 119, 121
Catherine of Alexandria, saint 53, 87–88
Catherine of Siena, saint 33
Cattaneo, Danese 10
Cellini, Benvenuto 7–8, 10, 118
Ceresara, Paride 57
Cesari, Antonio 8
Charles V, emperor 94, 101, 109
Charles VIII, king of France 26, 29
Chatfield, Mary P. 117
Chigi (Gisi), Agostino 41, 85, 89
Cian, Vittorio 118–21
Cittadini, Evangelista 68
Clemente VII, pope, *see* Medici, Giulio de'
Colón, Diego 66
Colonna, Francesco 20, 80
Colonna, Vittoria 57, 106, 109, 112
Columbus, Christopher 66
Contarini, Gasparo 10, 105–06, 108, 116
Conti, Sigismondo de' 83–84
Corner (family) 37, 59, 64
Corner, Andrea 59
Corner (Cornaro), Caterina, queen of Cyprus 37, 59–60, 63, 66
Corner, Giorgio 37
Correggio, Niccolò da 57
Cortese, Gregorio 112, 122
Cossa, Francesco del 30
Costa, Lorenzo 54, 57
Cranach, Lucas the Younger 9
Curti, Elisa 121
Cybo, Giovanni Battista 18

Danzi, Massimo ix, 118–19, 122
De Caprio, Vincenzo 121
Della Casa, Giovanni 4–5, 10, 20, 112, 118–19
Della Rovere, Francesco 16, 22, 72, 75, 89

Della Rovere, Francesco Maria I 72–73, 121
Della Rovere, Galeotto 72
Della Rovere, Giovani 72
Della Rovere, Giuliano 72, 82, 85, 88–89
Della Torre, Ambrogina Faustina 5, 10, 57, 95
Della Torre, Antonio 95
Della Torre, Mariola 95
Della Volta, Achille 4
De Nolhac, Pierre 122
Dilemmi, Giorgio 117
Dionisotti, Carlo, 47, 117–19
Di Teodoro, Francesco Paolo 119
Domitian 7
Donà, Girolamo 22, 25
Donata 45
Donnini, Andrea 118
Dovizi da Bibbiena, Bernardo 67, 89, 91–93, 120–21
Ducimetière, Nicolas ix

Erasmus of Rotterdam 27, 29, 36
Este, family 50
Este, Alfonso d' 14, 48, 50, 52, 72, 82, 120
Este, Isabella d' 48, 54, 57, 102, 120
Este, Niccolò III d' 19
Este, Leonello d' 29
Este, Ercole d' 20, 48, 52
Este, Ferrante d' 52
Este, Giulio d' 52
Este, Ippolito d' 52

Facino, Galeazzo 22
Faini, Marco 121
Farnese, Alessandro 50, 58, 89, 104–06, 109
Farnese, Alessandro (cardinal) 106, 122
Farnese, Giulia 50
Farnese, Pier Luigi 106, 109
Farnese, Ottavio 109
Favaro, Maiko 120
Felice 115
Ferrajoli, Alessandro 121
Ficino, Marsilio 17
Firpo, Massimo 122
Flaminio, Marco Antonio 108–09
Florisz, Adriaan 94–95
Fontanini, Benedetto 108
Fonte Avellana 73
Forcellino, Antonio 121
Fortunio, Giovan Francesco 97, 100
Fracastoro, Girolamo 105
Fragnito, Gigliola 122
Francis, saint 19
François I 109
Fra Giocondo *see* Giovanni Giocondo da Verona
Fregoso, Federico 22, 76, 83, 97, 106, 109, 116
Fregoso, Ottaviano 76–78

Gabriel (Gabriele), Angelo 23–25

Index

Gabriele, Trifone (Trifon) 30
Galen 29
Gambara, Veronica, 57
Gasparotto, Davide 118
Gerardo, Matteo
Gheri, Cosimo 95, 106, 108
Gheri, Filippo 109
Ghirlandaio, Domenico 19
Giannetto, Nella 119
Gibert, Caroline ix
Giberti (Ghiberto), Giovanni Matteo 4, 98, 100–01, 122
Giorgio da Castelfranco 68–69
Giorgione *see* Giorgio da Castelfranco
Giovanni Antonio 103
Giovanni Giocondo da Verona 21
Giovanni da Udine 106
Giustinian (di Candia), Giovanni 100
Giustiniani, Tommaso 14, 65, 67, 76, 119
Gnocchi, Alessandro 118–19
Gonzaga, family 50
Gonzaga, Cesare 77, 121
Gonzaga, Eleonora 72, 74
Gonzaga, Elisabetta 48, 57, 71–73, 76–77, 79, 82, 84, 117, 121
Gonzaga, Ercole 58
Gonzaga, Federico 68, 85
Gonzaga, Francesco II 57, 72
Gonzaga, Gian Francesco 68
Gonzaga, Margherita 85
Gorgias 25
Goro, Giusto 1, 2, 10, 95, 103
Goro, Simone 1
Gottfried, Rudolf B. 117
Gradenigo, Paolo 114
Gradenigo, Pietro 114
Griffo, Francesco 23
Griffoni, Maria *see* Savorgnan, Maria
Griffoni, Matteo 120
Gritti, Andrea 73, 104, 121
Gronau, Giorgio 121
Gualteruzzi, Carlo 122
Guardi, Francesco 2
Guarini, Guarino 29
Guicciardini, Francesco 26, 119

Henry VIII (Enrico VIII) 71, 121
Honorius III *see* Savelli, Cencio
Horace 33, 39

Inghirami, Tommaso (Fedra) 37–38
Innocent VIII, pope, *see* Cybo, Giovanni Battista

Jeanneret, Michel ix
Julius Caesar 7
Julius II, pope, *see* Della Rovere, Giuliano

Khayr al-Dīn, 109

Kidwell, Carol 118

Lascaris, Costantino 22–23, 25, 27, 119
Lastraioli, Chiara ix
Laurana, Luciano 71
Lawrence, saint 112–13
Leonardi, Giovanni Jacopo 73, 121
Leoniceno, Niccolò 29, 119
Leopardi, Giacomo 8
Leo X, pope, *see* Medici, Giovanni de'
Leto, Pomponio 26, 37, 39
Lombardo, Pietro 21
Lombardo, Tullio 21
Longueil, Christophe de 27
Lonigo, Niccolò da *see* Leoniceno, Niccolò
Loredan, Leonardo 93
Lorenzo il Magnifico *see* Medici, Lorenzo de'
Lotto, Lorenzo 60, 62
Louis XI, king of France 22
Louis XII, king of France 72
Lowe, Viviane ix
Luciani, Sebastiano 85, 107
Ludovic of Toulouse 60
Ludovico il Moro *see* Sforza, Ludovico
Ludovisi, family 68–69
Lusignan, Jacques de 59–60
Lusignan, James III de 59
Luther, Martin 108
Lutz, Maria 117
Luzio, Alessandro 120

Machiavelli, Niccolò 94
Mantegna, Andrea 7, 57
Manuzio, Aldo 20, 23, 25, 29, 31–33, 36, 46, 57, 119
Marcello, Elena 1, 2, 20, 108
Marchesi, Valentina 117
Margaret of Austria 109
Marsilio, Antonio 41
Martini, Francesco di Giorgio 71–72
Marullo, Michele 119
Massola, Elisabetta *see* Querini, Elisabetta
Maurolico, Francesco 36
Maximilian I, emperor 72
Medici, family 16, 26, 119
Medici, Giovanni de' 17, 36, 39–41, 88, 92, 94–95, 100, 119, 121
Medici, Giuliano de' (Magnifico Giuliano) 2, 3, 4, 31, 92, 97
Medici, Giuliano 16
Medici, Giulio de' 4, 17, 79, 101–02
Medici, Lorenzo de' 2, 16–17, 36, 64, 78
Medici, Piero di Lorenzo de' 26
Medici, Piero de' 25
Memling, Hans 21
Menega 44
Michiel, Marcantonio 41, 119
Molino, Antonio (il Burchiella) 68

Molza, Francesco Maria 116
Montefeltro, family 50
Montefeltro, Federico da 16, 71–72, 22
Montefeltro, Giovanna da 72
Montefeltro, Guidubaldo da 57, 71–73, 77, 82–84, 91, 117
More, Thomas 27
Morosina, *see* Della Torre, Ambrogina Faustina
Motta, Uberto 121
Myron 92

Navagero (Navaiero), Andrea 18, 21–22, 70, 89, 91, 102, 104, 105
Noniano 25, 56, 94, 99–100, 103, 112

Odasi, Lodovico 83
Ordeaschi, Francesca 85
Orlandi, Giovanni 119
Orsini, Fulvio 122
Ovid 85

Pacioli, Luca 21
Pagliaroli, Stefano 121
Paul, hermit 65
Paul, saint 109, 116
Paul II, pope, *see* Barbo, Paolo
Paul III, pope, *see* Farnese, Alessandro
Paul IV, pope, *see* Carafa, Giovan Pietro
Pazzi, family 16
Perin del Vaga *see* Buonaccorsi, Pietro
Perocco, Daria 117
Perotto, 64
Peruzzi, Baldassarre 85
Peter, saint 111
Peter Damian, saint 73
Petrarca (Petrarch), Francesco 17–18, 20, 30–35, 46–47, 55, 57, 66–67, 73, 79, 92, 119
Phidias 92
Piccolomini, Enea Silvio 22
Pico della Mirandola, Giovanni 18, 20, 26, 65
Pico della Mirandola, Giovan Francesco 36, 88
Piéjus, Marie-Françoise 117
Piero della Francesca *see* Piero di Benedetto de' Franceschi
Piero di Benedetto de' Franceschi 71
Pinturicchio *see* Bernardino di Betto Betti
Pio da Carpi family 100
Pio da Carpi, Alberto 20, 57
Pio da Carpi, Rodolfo 100
Pio da Carpi, Emilia 73, 77–79, 121
Piovego, river 9
Pirovano, Donato 120
Pisanello *see* Antonio di Puccio Pisano
Pius II, pope, *see* Piccolomini, Enea Silvio
Plautus 50
Pliny 29, 119
Podocataro, Livio 116, 122

Pole, Reginald 27, 89, 105–09, 116
Poliziano, Angelo *see* Ambrogini, Angelo
Pontano, Giovanni Gioviano 23, 28
Porto, Luigi da 103
Pozzi, Mario 117
Premuda, Loris 119
Prisciani, Pellegrino 30
Procaccioli, Paolo 122
Ptolemy 41

Querini, Elisabetta 112, 114, 122
Querini, Girolamo 115
Querini, Lorenzo *see* Querino, Piero
Querini, Piero 112, 114
Querini, Vincenzo 14, 37, 65, 67–68, 70, 119
Quondam, Amedeo 121

Raboni, Giulia 117–18
Ramberti, Benedetto 103
Ramusio, Giovanni Battista 21, 103, 119
Ravasco, Alfredo 50
Renée of France 102
Renier, Rodolfo 120
Riario, Raffaele 89
Roberti, Ercole de' 30
Romei, Danilo 122

Sabellico, Marco Antonio 22
Sadoleto, Jacopo 10, 82–83, 89, 105–06
Sangallo, Antonio da 89, 106
Sangallo, Giuliano da 89
Sannazaro, Jacopo 23, 105
Sansovino, Francesco 118
Santasofia, family 33
Sanudo, Leonardo 104
Sanudo, Marino 103–05
Sanvito, Bartolomeo 21, 23, 33
Sanzio, Raffaello 3, 4, 37–40, 58, 66, 73, 85–89, 91–93, 98, 106, 119, 121
Saul 110
Savelli, Cencio 19
Savoia, Bona 16
Savonarola, Girolamo 26, 33
Savorgnan, Giacomo 44
Savorgnan, Girolamo 18–19, 103
Savorgnan, Maria 31, 33, 43–47, 57, 95, 115, 117, 120
Sebastiano del Piombo, *see* Luciani, Sebastiano
Seidel Menchi, Silvana 119
Seneca 18, 37
Sermini, Nino 58
Sforza, Francesco 22
Sforza, Galeazzo Maria 16
Sforza, Gian Galeazzo 16, 26
Sforza, Giovanni 52
Sforza, Lucrezia 68
Sforza, Ludovico 26
Sforza, Ottaviano Maria 68

Shankland, Hugh 117
Simonetta, Cicco 16
Sixtus IV, pope, *see* Della Rovere, Francesco
Sole, Antonino 118
Soranzo, Vittore 103, 108–09, 122
Spira, Giovanni da 1
Straparola, Giovan Francesco 68, 70
Strozzi, Ercole 30–31, 33, 37, 50, 52, 97, 118
Strozzi, Tito Vespasiano 20
Suleiman I, Sultan 109
Superchio, Valerio 37

Tasso, Bernardo 97
Tasso, Torquato 97
Tebaldeo, Antonio 30, 39, 52, 57, 91, 93, 119
Tedaldi, family 17
Terence 17, 37, 118
Tiepolo, Niccolò 14, 82, 119
Titian, *see* Vecellio, Tiziano
Tomarozzo, Flaminio 58, 120
Tomeo, Niccolò Leonico 27
Travi, Ernesto 117
Trivigiano, Benedetto 68

Tura, Adolfo 118
Tura, Cosmè 30

Ubaldini, Ottaviano 72
Ulery, Robert W. Jr. 117
Urticio, Giovanni Alessandro 17

Varchi, Benedetto 8, 100, 118, 122
Vasari, Giorgio 89
Vecellio, Tiziano 10, 12, 73–75, 112–13, 121
Vela, Claudio 118, 121
Villa Bozza 9, 58, 114
Vinci, Leonardo da 21, 40, 57, 64, 88
Virgil 33, 36–37, 79, 118
Visconti, Gaspare 22
Vitruvius 21, 85, 92

Wilson, Nigel 118

Zaggia, Massimo 122
Zambotto, Bernardino 50, 120
Zapperi, Roberto 120

CPSIA information can be obtained
at www.ICGtesting.com
Printed in the USA
LVHW01n1638240118
563851LV00005B/60/P